COMING HOME

For All Who Dream of a New Church

C. Welton Gaddy
Author/Editor

Smyth & Helwys Publishing, Inc.®
Macon, Georgia

D1523529

ISBN 1-880837-95-1

Coming Home
Author/Editor
C. Welton Gaddy

©1995
Smyth & Helwys Publishing, Inc.®
Macon, Georgia

All biblical quotations are taken from the
New Revised Standard Version (NRSV) unless otherwise indicated.

All royalties derived from sales of this book
will go to Northminster Church in Monroe, Louisiana.

Library of Congress Cataloging-in-Publication Data
Gaddy, C. Welton.
    Coming Home / by C. Welton Gaddy.
    x + 154 pp.   6" x 9" (15 x 23 cm.)
    Includes bibliographical references.
    ISBN 1-880837-95-1
    1. Northminster Church (Monroe, La.)
    2. Southern Baptist Convention—History—20th century.
    3. Baptists—Lousiana—History—20th century.
    4. Church development, New—Baptists.
    5. Monroe (La.)—Church history—20th century.
    6. Louisiana—Church history—20th century.
    7. Choice of church.
    I. Title.
    BX6462.5.M66G33   1995   94-3587
    286'.1763—dc20   CIP

Contents

Preface vii
Acknowledgments ix
Introduction 1

I. Wandering 7

1. Free at Last! 15
   David A. Farmer
2. Journey Without Map 21
   Lynda Weaver-Williams

II. Becoming 29

3. The Church in the New Testament 40
   Frank Stagg
4. Our Vocation: The Ministry of Reconciliation 48
   Frank Stagg
5. Three Eternal Questions for the Church and Individual . . . 53
   Sarah Frances Anders

III. Meeting 59

6. Overcoming Obstacles to Inclusion 63
   Stan Hastey
7. Let God Be God 72
   Michelle Toole

IV. Possessing 79

8. Impulse to Venture and Security 90
   Frank Stagg
9. Churches and Church Houses 94
   Frank Stagg
10. Wooden Tongues and Hungry Ears 99
    James Lamkin

V. Hurting 105

   11. Life Together 113
               Nancy Hastings Sehested

VI. Celebrating 119

   12. Sketching a Vision 129
               C. Welton Gaddy
   13. Coming Home 134
               C. Welton Gaddy
   14. Shepherds and Sheep 143
               Frank Stagg

Epilogue: Living at Home 151

Preface

Some books are birthed with great pain. An author struggles to find a good idea and wrestles with that idea trying to discover a way to express it that is at least interesting, if not enlightening and entertaining. Discipline dominates every stage of the writing process. Recording thoughts on paper is hard work that the author considers a demanding chore.

Other books take form by way of a process abounding with pleasure. An idea captivates an author, refusing to let go of her until she has placed on paper words that have been dancing in her mind. The author does not have to labor to make the material interesting, only to tell a story that, by its very nature, is intriguing. Little discipline is required to complete such a manuscript. Writing takes on the nature of fun.

This book falls into (or arises out of) the second category. Over the course of a few days, a story gripped me, demanding to be told and promising to be beneficial when it was told. I tried to free myself from the grip of this impulse to write in order to devote my attention to other concerns. The story, the ideas it embraces, and its promise would not turn loose of me, however. So, finally, I gave in to it—not fretfully, but happily. Cecil Staton and Scott Nash encouraged me.

The narrative that follows comes from long hours of pleasurable listening; so do the sermons and other worship materials included in this volume. Numerous individuals have recounted for me their own personal stories while retracing the larger story of their (our) family of faith. As I heard numerous references to a particular worship service, sermon, litany, anthem, or prayer considered pivotal to the encouragement and direction of the Northminster Church fellowship, I sought out copies of those materials and read them or listened to them.

I found listening to people's stories of pilgrimage to be as inspiring as it was enlightening. So, pulling together the right words to get this material on paper was a welcome challenge.

A professor of history in our church reminded me that the real nature of some events simply cannot be captured in words. He was right, of course; but without descriptive words, however inadequate, those events may never be known at all. If only a few individuals who read the words that follow can sense even minimally the excitement that energized a group of people who stumbled into a vision of something new, the enthusiasm that propelled these people to bring their God-shaped dream into reality, and the commitment that called forth these people's sacrificial efforts to maintain a structure that approximates the nature of a New Testament church and to minister to all people in a manner that conjures up thoughts of home, then the pleasure I have known in telling the story will be enhanced even more. If God can use these words to encourage other people to embark upon new initiatives of grace and give themselves to the formation of fellowships of mercy, my joy in writing will be complete.

C. Welton Gaddy

Acknowledgments

Late one cold, winter evening, while seated on a floor in front of a wood-burning stove that was overheating, I engaged in a free wheeling, gut-level-honest discussion with a group of young people from Northminster Church, the fellowship I had begun to serve as pastor several weeks earlier. These young people and I had traveled to a cabin set in the midst of a camp constructed for hunters and fishers so we could become better acquainted with each other. After talking for a while about our church, I asked my new friends a question that I thought would prompt an important revelation of feelings: "If you could say anything you want to say to the adults in Northminster Church, what would you say?" After a brief period of silent searching, Amanda Joiner said, "Thank you. I would say 'thank you' to them."

I was stunned. I had asked this question to other church groups of young people in the past, but none had ever given this response. Before I could ask why, others in the group were nodding their heads in agreement. Some were speaking: "I would thank them for going through what they have gone through to provide us the kind of church we have." "I would thank them for including us in every meeting and activity of the church since the first day we met." "I would thank them for letting us participate in worship as leaders and especially for allowing us to help serve communion."

Who said what, I do not remember—Laura or Leslie Smallwood, Reese Pearson, Liner or Larkin Gibbs, Leigh Pierce, Richard Bryan, Brodie or Cameron Glenn. All of them were in agreement regarding their gratitude for Northminster Church. That late evening gab session confirmed my decision to find time to listen to the story of this congregation and to write that story down.

Don Nixon, Associate Pastor and Minister of the Arts in Northminster Church, has been an invaluable resource person in this project. I am not sure who has had the most fun—Don relating stories from the church's early days or me listening to them. As Don and I talked all one afternoon about my desire to do this book, he encouraged me and offered helpful suggestions. I believe he first had the idea of using the pilgrimage of the people of Israel as a prototype for discussing the journey of Northminster Church. Almost daily, I have gone to Don with questions that he appeared to welcome and to which he responded with comprehensive information.

Several people in the Northminster congregation have set patiently in my office and allowed me to quiz them at length about what they could remember regarding the inception and development of this congregation. Don and Cathe Nixon, Craig Henry, Priscilla Asbury, and Kay Southern have read the historical sections of this manuscript and offered corrections as well as additional beneficial information. Any errors still present, however, are mine, not theirs.

The only sadness I feel as I write these words of gratitude is that I cannot mention the name of every person in the church. Each member is a vital part of the story and merits recognition.

Words of appreciation are in order also for the numerous people who have led workshops and worship services at Northminster Church, who allowed me to see notes, if not manuscripts, of their presentations. Space limitations have prevented the inclusion of more of these works in this volume. I am especially grateful to the persons whose sermons appear on the following pages. They have cooperated with me and consented for their work to be published apart from any financial remuneration.

As always, I am grateful for my wife Judy and appreciative for her encouragement to write as well as her insistence on taking times away from writing (which make writing even more enjoyable).

Finally, I am thankful to and for the people who are Northminster Church. I am grateful to God for working in and through these people to create a story that is as inspiring as it is interesting.

Introduction

Coming home is an absolutely wonderful experience, an experience unequaled by any other. What joy erupts when a person arrives at home after having been away for so long that she had begun to wonder if she would ever get back home! How indescribably good it is to find a home if you never really had a home, but always desperately wanted one! Happiness knows no limits for a man who discovers a home after once having a home, eventually losing it, and ultimately concluding that he never would know the joy of home life again. When people who have been so disappointed by empty promises about home purveyed by boastful imposters of families that they finally decide home is no more than an idyllic wish find the real thing, words cannot capture the sensation of peace and happiness that they experience.

To come home is to discover our true family—matriarchs and patriarchs whose passionate love focuses on our best interests, brothers and sisters in the spirit. Our kin are our friends and vice versa. At home we are surrounded by colleagues in mercy, joint heirs of promise, and fellow pilgrims.

To come home is to be overwhelmed by or swept up in a rush of emotions that makes us want to do everything—a lot of different things —at once: to dash to our favorite place for retreat and solitude, to stand under the old apple tree in the backyard and look up into the sky through its branches, to rummage through the wooden chest that we once made the repository of our keepsakes and memorabilia, to sit at the kitchen table and attempt to conjure up the aroma of fresh summer vegetables cooking on the stove, to relax in a recliner by the fireplace, to run up and down the stairs to see if the step next to the bottom still squeaks, to gaze out every window in the house to see what all has changed. Unable to do anything because of wanting to do everything, we dry the tears from our eyes and breathe a prayer, thanking God for the experience of coming home.

This book is about coming home. It is not about returning to a birth place or taking up residence in a specific location. This is a story about people finding a fellowship that is more like home than any ever dared to think was possible. More than that, it is a story about people who *are* home.

The coming home experience that dominates this story is more spiritual than physical, more relational than geographical. It is about love, grace, faith, and hope rather than about nails, lumber, bricks, and mortar.

I wish I could write that the discoveries of home described on the following pages occurred at the end of an intense, intentional journey in which people knew precisely what they were looking for, set out to discover it, and immediately knew when they found it. That is not the case, however.

The big story in this book is made up of many individual stories, each story differing from the others. What most of the people I am writing about held in common did not seem like much at first—disappointment, rejection, bitterness, and anger. But when they looked more closely, they discovered a mutual commitment to holding faith with integrity, living with a faint hope, and loving each other. These folks bonded together and started moving in a direction of mission without any earthly idea of the involvements into which it would lead them. Along the way, they developed a sense of family. Eventually, they knew they had come home.

Recently, I have met a lot of homeless people, spiritually speaking. Their comments comprise a litany of pathos:

• No one understands me.

• I feel like nobody accepts me for who I am.

• I turned to the people whom I thought would help me, and they hurt me instead of helping.

• I feel like a stranger everywhere I go, even in church.

• I no longer know a place where I feel at home.

Why? What has happened? No one reason explains the enormous number of people currently adrift in pain. In some instances, individuals have created problems that caused alienation and a sense of isolation. In other instances, people have been disenfranchised by problems over which they had no control. In both situations, the people involved should still have had a home to which they could turn, but that was not the case. An elderly gentleman speaks out of obvious anger and bitterness:

> My church was stolen! A new breed of minister used a flood of holy talk to get elected as our pastor. Then, immediately, he altered all our church policies, replacing congregationalism with a hierarchy capped by pastoral authoritarianism. This audacious young man recruited people devoted to him rather than to the church, and now the church is theirs— his. I no longer have a church home.

A young woman explains between sobs:

> I made the decision to get a divorce fully aware that permanent marriage is the biblical goal. With God's help, I did what appeared to be the best (and the right) thing to do in a bad situation. But, now my church relegates me to the status of a second-class citizen. I am welcome to attend worship and encouraged to give an offering, but I am regularly reminded that I can't really be at home in this fellowship.

A university student tells me,

> I feel so disoriented and displaced. Through the programs of the Baptist Student Union on my campus, I got in touch with the leadership of God and experienced a divine call to serve as a pastoral minister. Now, though, my home church tells me I must be confused. They refuse to recognize my call and ordain me to the ministry. I don't have any place to go where I can be at home.

A former pastor pours out his heart,

> I was accused of taking money that was not mine. I didn't do it. I was in a situation in which a few people perceived that I did wrong. Then they came at me with that old 'perception is reality' line. Finally, several of the people admitted that they knew I was innocent of my wrongdoing. But, this was their chance to get rid of me and bring in someone they could more tightly control. So, they dismissed me and labeled me. Now, no church wants to touch me. What am I to do about my call from God that remains real and my will to be a messenger of

grace? I can't find a church that will even hire me, much less call me
to experience it as a new home.

Spiritual and ecclesiastical homelessness has reached crisis propor-
tions among many persons once integrally involved in the Southern
Baptist Convention. The fallout of the power struggle within this national
body includes fragmentation, disillusionment, anger, hurt, and schism that
forcefully impact local congregations and individual persons, leaving
them without a sense of home.

Especially hard hit by recent convention battles are women who want
to do pastoral ministry, homosexuals who want recognition as a part of
a church family, and individuals who refuse to parrot a creedal statement
about the Bible as a substitute for confessing their belief in the Bible.
Others adversely affected by what has been called "the fundamentalist
take-over" include laypersons who want to practice their God-given
priesthood in churches committed to the sole authority of the pastor;
scholars who wish to pursue truth without restrictions; teachers who want
to encourage learning and not engage in catechetical indoctrination; people who desire a complete separation between biblical faith and partisan
politics; and individuals who really believe that "where the spirit of the
Lord is, there is freedom."

A collage of comments from a variety of individuals dramatizes the
severity of the plights of those who are homeless:

• I no longer recognize the denominational institutions to which
I formerly looked for inspiration, guidance, and instruction.

• I go to the same church that I have been a member of for
thirty-five years, but I no longer feel like I belong. Everything
has changed. Entertainment has replaced worship. Policy decisions are announced rather than discussed. All that anybody
seems to want to do is grow, and apparently nobody cares how
we do it.

• I can no longer count on experiencing meaningful worship in
my church. Preaching has degenerated into a loud harangue. The
great music of our faith has been set aside for tunes that sound
like advertisement jingles. People are more into clapping their

hands than praying. Recently, the pastor advised us that he didn't want any music in worship that didn't cause us to pat our feet. "If you can't hum it, don't use it" were his words. Where can I go to worship as a member of the family of God?

God does a surprising amount of good with very bad situations. This truth has been readily apparent since the divinely-orchestrated exodus of Israel from Egypt. Nowhere was it ever clearer than in God's ability to transform a hideous crucifixion in the Middle East into an event of cosmic redemption. Now, God is at it again.

Out of the denominational turmoil of recent years, the conflicts that have arisen in local congregations, and the sense of spiritual homelessness that has shrouded so many individuals, God is shaping new families of faith and creating novel structures for faith development. New visions are generating influential missions. Fellowships dedicated to inclusiveness are developing. The gospel is being proclaimed apart from the prejudices and traditions of certain mindsets and particular cultures.

Involvement in new initiatives can be scary at first. Friends do not understand the impatience with old ways and eagerness to try something better. Criticism abounds. Enemies proliferate. "The establishment" plasters the new venturers with labels aimed at raising suspicion about them and nurturing a fear of them. In the midst of suspicion and hurt, however, certainty develops: "God is in this; we are doing right."

This book contains the story of just such a group of people and their new initiative in worship and ministry. I am writing the story because I want to affirm and encourage these people, and because many people have requested a reporting of this story. My account is for them as well. Then, too, many other individuals and groups need this story.

My hope is that a recounting of one group's journey home will inspire a similar pilgrimage among others. I know individuals so fed up with their churches that they have given up on the possibility of a meaningful church fellowship. By way of this volume, I want to say to them, "Don't do it. Don't give up. Alternatives exist."

Maybe this story will strike a fire that flames into courage among people who sit passively and dejectedly among old, meaningless structures, when, if they would only get up and get out, they could live on the front edge of God's redemptive mission in contemporary society. Just because something has not been done, that does not mean something cannot be done. God can use the kind of people who will read this book to establish new structures of grace.

The journey is not an easy one. In reality, the journey may not always lead you where you think it will. But along the way, you will know the joy of the journey and the peace of God's presence as you travel. All who sense that peace and joy will begin to see each other as family. Sooner or later, whether you have arrived at where you want to be or you are still going, you will have this sensation of coming home.

There is nothing else in the world like it. Coming home is an absolutely wonderful experience!

I.
Wandering

"We journeyed into the wilderness."
(Deut 2:1)

"If your presence will not go, do not carry us up from here. For how shall it be known that I have found favor in your sight, I and your people unless you go with us? In this way, we shall be distinct, I and your people, from every people on the face of the earth."

(Exod 33:15-16)

"We walk by faith, not by sight."
(2 Cor 5:7)

Betrayed. Uprooted. Displaced. Angry. Hurt. Lost. Disoriented. Sad. Numb. Such feelings can kill a spirit of venture, inspire cynicism, stagnate personal growth, and justify giving up on the institution or activity that has caused the negative emotions—but not in every instance. I know a small fellowship of Christians for whom precisely these potentially-destructive feelings served as the inspiration for a journey into spiritual renewal, a search that wound its way into an authentic community of grace and an excited sprint toward hope.

Late in November 1988, one week before Advent, a beleagured group of Christian believers in Monroe, Louisiana, gathered in Kay Southern's house on the banks of Bayou Desiard for conversation, fellowship, and worship. Seven days later the holy season of patient waiting and joyful expectation would begin. But, how would these pilgrims experience Advent this year? How *could* they take the journey into hope without a church? On the following Thursday, these individuals would be expected to celebrate Thanksgiving Day with their families and friends. How, though? On this Sunday afternoon, gratitude was in short supply among them. Anxiety, impatience, and grief were plentiful.

Four days prior to this gathering, a series of actions with wide ranging implications in their church life had shocked many of these people and filled them with gross disappointments. Numbness followed, though anger hurriedly rushed in to set their emotions on edge. Some of the individuals who were present on that Sunday afternoon remember vividly the negative feelings that churned in their souls and shook their spirits at the time. Others, even after prolonged reflection, cannot fully describe the fierce storms that attacked their spiritual security and threatened to devastate long-held convictions.

A sizable number of people who had been long-term members of the same church (several of them were lifelong members of this congregation) suddenly found themselves without a church. Sounds of applause rang in their ears and ripped at their hearts—hand clapping that erupted among other members of their former congregation when, during a Wednesday evening business meeting, a few individuals requested that their names be removed from the church's roll as an act of protest against a major decision made by the church.

Devoted church people for virtually all of their lives, these people realized they no longer had a church home. Instinctively they turned to each other. Soon they knew they were not alone. Then came support from unexpected places. Friends from different parts of the city of Monroe, some who were members of other churches and some who had long ago given up on the institutional church, reached out to these hurting people with compassion, even if without a complete understanding of their situation.

More importantly—actually, *most* importantly—these religiously homeless folks sensed God's presence in their midst. Several of the individuals later confessed that from the very beginning they had felt that God was about to do something special with them.

Each of the twenty-five or thirty people who filed into the living room of the Southern household on that wintry, November afternoon had very personal reasons for being there. None of the individuals could deny the negative feelings that throbbed within them. Why should they? One woman spoke of the hurt inflicted by severely fractured relationships with persons to whom she had been a friend for scores of years. Another lady indicated that after being faithfully involved in a church for all of her life, she suddenly felt displaced, devoid of a church. Several individuals talked of being in shock. Harold Hughens, a veteran, widely-respected minister, recalls, "I felt like I had been abused."

Grief seared the spirits of the people who gathered in Kay Southern's living room, but not one of them arrived there eager to spend a Sunday afternoon observing a wake. Surprisingly few of the people present harbored much interest in spending a significant amount of time looking backward. The future had to be considered. They were ready to get on with it.

A sense of unity and intimacy developed among these people with mind-boggling rapidity. Diverse needs among individuals gave way to mutually shared needs among the group, most prominent of which were a need to be with loving people and a need to worship God. The result was a community of people tightly bonded to each other and unalterably dedicated to the meaningful worship of Almighty God.

Priscilla Asbury and Craig Henry planned the worship experience for that first Sunday afternoon and brought a printed order of worship to the meeting. After the Bible reading and a hymn, Craig quoted freely from Harry Emerson Fosdick's sermon on finding God in strange or unlikely places. This band of wanderers was in an unlikely place. They desperately wanted to celebrate the reality of God's presence among them.

Cognizant of pervasive hurt among the worshipers and the need for an experience of intimacy, Craig Henry suggested that Christian communion be made the focal point of the afternoon meeting. Hannah Clark brought a glass pitcher to the service, and Kay Southern provided a brass cup. Gathered around a coffee table, against the backdrop of a fire that Dick Fuchs had made in the fireplace, this group of wounded pilgrims shared a broken loaf of bread and a common cup of wine in Jesus' name.

No one person had to say, "Let's do this again." Unspoken unanimity on this point preceded any words. Everyone present seemed to agree with Priscilla Asbury that the afternoon worship service together was the "absolutely right thing to do."

The worship service for the next Sunday was scheduled for the Southern house at 11:00 A.M. Gone was any worry about that time conflicting with the worship schedule of any other church. These worshipers knew they belonged together. As word of their meeting spread during the ensuing week, other people decided to become a part of this venture of faith.

On the first Sunday of Advent, none of this small band of people gathered for worship where they had planned to meet a month earlier. But given the recent developments in their pilgrimage of faith, every one of them was where they wanted to be on this Sunday immediately following Thanksgiving Day—together—together to worship the God of promise and hope. Sitting in Kay Southern's living room again, the worshipers listened to an audio tape recording of Carlyle Marney's sermon "A Priest at Every Elbow" and then shared communion.

Communion quickly became the most crucial event in worship for this group of people. Within the shared bread and common cup were all of the spiritual truths needed during a period of struggle. Religiously speaking, these people had nothing left in their lives except God. They had been stripped of all institutional resources and left adrift to find a religious path for themselves, but on the table before them were bread and wine from God, like manna and water in the desert. Here were the body and blood of Christ. Here was the promise of life in the midst of the reality of death. Here was a meal of hope consumed in a context of betrayal. Communion was all they needed. Each of the worshipers knew that God was present and, as of old, providing nourishment for people wandering through a wilderness.

Taking seriously the biblical truth elaborated so convincingly in Carlyle Marney's sermon, members of this small but rapidly enlarging group of people became priests to each other. Since they had no professional staff of ministers to assist them, and at this point absolutely no desire for one, each person assumed a role of ministry. Some handled logistical concerns, others worship planning, and still others pastoral care. Members

of the congregation took turns serving communion. "That was strange,"
one lady recalls. "We had always depended on an ordained minister to
serve communion."

In Kay Southern's house, a balcony overlooks the living room on
three sides. In each corner of the fourth side of the room, a winding stair-
way leads to the balcony. When worship began during the third meeting
of this new fellowship, a choir lined the steps rising above the living
room and, under the direction of Don Nixon, the singers lifted their voices to sing the music of the season.

The first preacher to address this small, remarkably close-knit band
of worshipers was William Hodge, a minister from Birmingham, Alabama, who was visiting in Monroe. On the Sunday of Advent traditionally
associated with peace, this guest preacher comforted members of the new
congregation and challenged them regarding their responsibility for
peacemaking. William Hodge's prophetic words ring as true now as they
did during that emotion-laden moment in which he first spoke them:

> Who you will be in one year and five years and twenty years will
> be determined today in the throws of your birth, and how you make
> peace with the strife and torment of your genesis. There is no such
> thing as birth and growth without conflict. The sister of growth is con-
> flict. In conflict, there is always the possibility of growth.
>
> Families don't mature without conflict. In a real sense, you are the
> maturing sons and daughters of your spiritual family. It's time to leave
> your birth home and begin a family of your own, and parents have a
> hard time with children who want to be different.
>
> As your friend and guest, may I suggest that you make peace with
> your past and with yourselves, and with your spiritual mothers and fa-
> thers who have not come with you.
>
> Be faithful to your beliefs and convictions, and joy in the goodness
> of being different without the need to scorn those who might not under-
> stand or accept you.
>
> One sign of maturity is not having to be understood by everybody.
>
> Your spiritual parents may never bless you, but they may come to
> see and appreciate your bravery of launching out on your own to be-
> come what God has called you to be.

Individuals who were in attendance at the third meeting of this new
fellowship continue to speak of the moving moment when seventy-four

year-old Joyce Loftin extended the bread of communion with trembling hands and said to each worshiper in a shaky voice, "This is the body of Christ." Joyce recalls the event as well—the first time she ever served communion—especially how she kept asking herself, "Am I worthy to be holding this representation of the body of Christ?" After answering her question negatively, Joyce experienced a rush of assurance, "But God loves us though we're not worthy."

By Christmas, the number of people gathering each week to worship together had outgrown the Southern living room. The site for the congregation's corporate worship services was moved to the extra large great room in the house of D. H. and Hanna Clark. Sunday School classes were organized and assigned a meeting place in the Clark's residence. Though D. H. was serving as the director of music in another congregation in the city at the time, he offered invaluable assistance by planning the weekly worship services. Marj Stricklin, a pianist for twenty-one years in another congregation in the city, joined the fellowship (of which she said, "This baby has been waiting to be born for ten years") and began assisting in worship as an instrumentalist (a tenure that stretches into the present). Priscilla Asbury continued to prepare a printed order of worship for each Sunday. Guest preachers were invited to speak in the corporate services.

On the Friday evening prior to Christmas, 23 December 1988, D. H. Clark and Vickie Krutzer led the congregation in a meaningful service of lessons and carols. Joy was replacing sadness. Theology was becoming experience. God was at work in the world. Christ was being born anew.

A few people had dared to talk openly about the possibility of forming a new church. After all, the subject was not a totally novel one. Years earlier there had been talk of such a development. Craig Henry had voiced the conviction most recently. Movement toward becoming a church was more evident in actions than in declarations, however.

Priscilla Asbury remembers, "We were a people possessed." Harold Hughens reflects on the nature of the possession. "Leaving home is painful. We were born out of the pain of loss." Likening what happened to this group to the dynamics within a family, Harold observed, "We had to leave home to become who we are. Negative emotions provided energy to move toward images of church we had envisioned for years."

The pilgrims were moving—intentionally, excitedly, purposefully, and worshipfully. Amazement and awe accompanied each of their steps forward. Don Nixon concisely captured the nature of the developments that prompted such great surprises and unparalleled satisfaction among members of this family of faith, "People who controlled everything were suddenly out of control and being used by God."

1.
Free at Last

John 8:31-38
Deuteronomy 15:12-18

David Albert Farmer

(While serving as the pastor of Saint Charles Avenue Baptist Church in New Orleans, Louisiana, David Albert Farmer drove to Monroe to encourage and preach for Northminster Church on 21 May 1989. Dr. Farmer is presently the pastor of University Baptist Church in Baltimore, Maryland, and the editor of Pulpit Digest.*)*

In the musical, *Big River*, Jim is a slave. He wants desperately to be free, and—though I cannot understand any of the feelings or dynamics of being owned by another human being—I feel very deeply moved and somehow related to his experience when he sings:

> I wish by golly I could spread my wings and fly
> And let my grounded soul be free for just a little while
> To be like eagles when they ride upon the wind
> And taste the sweetest taste of freedom for my soul
> I'd be free at last, free at last
> Great God Almighty, I'd be free at last.[1]

These words probably stir up deep feelings for you too. I wonder what it is from which we contemporary folk want most to be free. There are modern slaveries from which people like us want to be delivered.

Perhaps the most obvious example of modern slavery is worry. We want to be free from worry. This is a theoretical statement, of course, and perhaps a statement of ideal. We all know those who—though they never could admit it—thrive on worry. Most people really would like to be rid of it and all its causes, however.

Naturally, we do not want to worry about having our basic physical needs met—needs for food, shelter, safety, clothing. Many people in our world never have a sphere of worry beyond this, but we do, so our worries are more luxurious though still very real.

We would like to be free from worry about unreasonable expectations. This baggage of unreasonable expectations must be related to a fear of failure or maybe of not achieving in such a way as to please society in general.

Consider the issue of whether or not a young mother should work outside her home. So many times, before she ever gets to the point of making her own decision, she must deal with the expectations of many others. She feels first the evident insignificance with which our culture at large seems to regard the housewife/mother role. She feels the pressure to add to the family income and keep alive her professional skills. Is there any way to please herself and all the rest? No.

When we talk about unrealistic self-expectations and the fear of failure, it becomes clear that "failure," a good bit of the time, means not living up to what someone else sets as a goal for us. Some of us get so hooked into this kind of living that we continue to worry about pleasing persons who have long since died. We could not please the dearly departed when he was alive, and we certainly cannot please her from the great beyond as his memory becomes even more untarnished and her will for our lives is, therefore, harder than ever to challenge. Though we may choose to keep on living for others like this, deep in our hearts we want to be free from it all because—though we cannot always affirm it—only *we*, in communion with God, can know what is best and right for us.

Most of us measure our value and the value of the jobs we perform in terms of material means. If we are not making good money in comparison to others we know who do jobs similar to ours or who are in our age brackets, we tend to worry and feel badly about ourselves.

Compensation reminds us that we find ourselves caught up in oppressive employment conditions—white collar types, assembly line types, and everything in-between. We know if we are not producing in a way that pleases a supervisor or a clientele, even when we are doing well, our job is in jeopardy. We are worried. We may give in to another's whims just to get along, even when we feel overloaded and/or dehumanized in the process.

How about health worries? This is a burdensome area for many persons, not just hypochondriacs. Think about how much more we modern persons know of possible health problems than did our forebears. While we are more informed—and certainly more healthy—because of publicity about hospitals and brochures in doctors' offices and doctors turned T.V. stars, all of the information that is as handy as everyday conversation can become the basis for worry and anxiety about our physical well-being.

It would be nice to be free from that kind of worry and all worry. We modern folks also want to be free from pain. We would like to be delivered from physical pain. It may not rob us of life, but it can certainly intrude and interrupt. All of us would want to be free from everything that goes along with this captivity because we want to love life.

We do not want physical or emotional pain. There are all kinds of emotional pain; a pervading one is guilt. We would be free from guilt's pain. Nearly every one of us has failed to be and to do what is right in some circumstances and relationships, either through omission or commission. Some of us take the guilt we feel for our failure and let it help us learn and make new plans for the future, but some of us have become slaves to guilt.

I mention Jim from *Big River* again. When his little daughter was quite young, Jim had become so angry at her that he gave her a severe beating. As a result, she would not mind him when he repeatedly told her to do some simple task such as close a door. Only afterwards did he find out that sickness had taken her hearing, and the little girl had not understood what he was saying to her. Years later, and long since separated from her, Jim had never gotten over that. His song was almost a prayer, and he meant it in the depths of his soul when he sang about freedom that might "let my feelings lie where harm cannot come by and hurt this always hurtin' heart that needs to rest a while."[2] You know just how he felt, though for reasons that may be quite different.

Furthermore, modern women and men would be free from all reminders of our finitude. The reality that we will not be around forever is most painful, and we try to pretend that earthly life is without end. Paradoxically, freedom can come only one way, and most of us do not want to pay the price. The only hope for this freedom is to face the truth: the reality that the length of earthly life is limited. Until we face that head on, we are slaves to our own mortality with all the uneasiness that is multiplied with it.

We want to be free from worry and free from pain. We also would be free from meaninglessness. One way of responding to the threat of meaninglessness is through the denial of reality. More and more of us, and those younger and younger among us, are relying on addictive substances and behaviors to cover the world in which we no longer find meaning. We do not want to be slaves to substances and habits, but often we are. Bad decisions over a long period of time, the pressures of everyday home and professional or school demands, emotional difficulties that we have not dealt with—all of these and more can cause us to become dependent on some substance or unhealthy way of acting as coping devices. Over time we wish we could be free of what has now come to control us.

Getting high frees us from reality for a time, though real freedom will not come from escape; freedom comes only in altering our world, or at least our perception of our world. I am talking about bad habits with addictions because I think they become utilized for the same reasons that substances are abused—namely, escape from reality. Psychiatrist Scott Peck points out that "almost all of us from time to time seek to avoid—in ways that can be quite subtle—the pain of assuming responsibility for our own problems."[3]

In the very profound and disturbing movie *The Mission*, Rodrigo Mendosa begins as a womanizer, mercenary, slave-trader of South American Indians, and murderer. He killed his own brother when the brother fell in love with a woman whom Mendosa himself professed to love. After the murder, Mendosa came to hate himself and gave up on life; he sat in a cell, not eating, wasting away. A conversation with Father Gabriel gave him hope that would ultimately bring meaning back to his life in spite of his gross failures.

In the cell, Father Gabriel asks, "Is this the way you mean to go on?" Mendosa replies, "There is nothing else." Father Gabriel counters, "There is life. There is a way out, Mendosa." Mendosa insists, "For me there is no redemption." Then Father Gabriel explains, "God gave us the burden of freedom; you chose your crime. Do you have the courage to choose your penance?"[4] Mendosa subsequently became a Jesuit priest and martyr of sorts.

God gave us the burden of freedom. Do we have the courage to make responsible, freeing choices, and when we fail to choose again? We are not slaves as Jim was a slave, but we can become enslaved—sometimes through no fault of our own, at other times precisely through our own poor and unhealthy choices. Whatever the cause, when we lose or give up our freedom, we long to be free. Some kind of freedom seems to be the yearning of the human spirit.

I wonder if this is related to the legal specification in our Old Testament lesson in Deuteronomy. The concern of this law is for the Israelite who had to sell himself into servitude in payment for a bad debt. It does not attempt to speak to all kinds or aspects of slavery; nonetheless, it is instructive. This material is in a larger section that has to do with the sabbatical year.

In the sabbatical year, the ancient Israelites were to release any indentured servants in their households. The owners also were to make sure that when the former slaves went out to freedom, they were to do so with enough material wealth to start a life for themselves: some livestock, grain, and wine. The owners were to do this on the basis of two facts: (1) The ancestors of these owners had once been slaves in Egypt but had been redeemed or liberated by God, and (2) God had blessed these owners with the material blessings they were able to enjoy; this same God loved the slaves no less.

Here we have evidence of the fact that God desires freedom for God's people. This is not an isolated or unusual example in the biblical literature. We do not have to wonder much at all about the broad elements in the foundation of God's will for us. This is but one piece of evidence that God wants us to be free people—not in economic slavery, but also not in the modern kinds of slavery: enslavement to worry, pain, and meaninglessness.

In ancient Israel people had no choice except to be slaves or go to prison for their debts. Their owners might have kept them in this position on and on, debating the terms of the agreement or by saying that their work had not been satisfactory. In the sabbatical year, the application of the law was—regardless of circumstances—if you owned indentured slaves you let them go free and helped them get a fresh start as free women and men. I am mighty proud to know a God who thinks freedom is a basic goal in human life.

Getting to the more emotional and spiritual levels of freedom and God's responses to these, we look to God's Son, our Lord, Jesus Christ. In the Fourth Gospel, we have these words from Jesus: "If you obey my teaching (if you continue in my word), you are really my disciples; you will know the truth, and the truth will make you free" (John 8:31-32 TEV). Jesus was talking to some Jewish people who had given intellectual assent to what he taught; that, of course, was and is only the beginning of a relationship with him. Thus, there was more to say. Jesus went on to point to the basis of the true and mature relationship with him that resulted in freedom. It involved both knowing or understanding and acting.

The acting was obedience to Jesus' teaching, responding in action to the implications of what Jesus taught about life in relationship to God: namely, if we are slaves to sin (that is, to the decision over and over again to please ourselves rather than God), we are not by our choice part of the household of God, and we are not free.

In his sermon, "The Truth Shall Make You Free," theologian Paul Tillich, asked how we grasp the truth that Jesus said would make us free.

> "By *doing* it," is the answer of the fourth gospel. This does not mean
> merely being obedient to the commandments, accepting them and ful-
> filling them. Doing the truth means living out of the reality which is *he*
> who is the truth, making his being the being of ourselves and of our
> world.[5]

Otherwise we are indentured servants who continue to sell ourselves to sin and slavery; we are in bondage, and after a break like a sabbatical year, we sell out again. When we have before us the possibility of libera-tion or redemption, we refuse it.

In contrast, though, if we choose the way of truth, if we live out God's will, then we are clearly children of God and part of the family that is precisely what Jesus meant when he said, "If the Son makes you free, you will be free indeed." As William Hull said, "The truth about which Jesus spoke is not a set of timeless ideas but a dynamic power that can make people free."[6]

How can we realize this? Tillich explained it this way:

> The truth which liberates is the power of love, for God is love. . . .
> Therefore, distrust every claim for truth where you don't see truth unit-
> ed with love and be certain that you are of the truth and that the truth
> has taken hold of you only when *love* has taken hold of you.[7]

Freedom causes us to take seriously God's love that keeps us away from the repetition of bad decisions that enslave us. Even when we are bound by circumstances beyond our control that would do everything to take away our physical freedom, freedom of the spirit can still prevail.

We are called today to freedom as people of God. It is a practical freedom, but it is first spiritual freedom. It is based on truth: the truth of God's love for all of us that invites us into continuing relationship with God, truth so real as to guide us into responsible decisions and so pervasive that we live it. Then we sing,

> Free at last, free at last
> Great God Almighty,
> I'm free at last![8]

Endnotes

[1]Roger Miller, "Free at Last," (Tree Publishing Co., 1985). Used by permission.

[2]Ibid.

[3]Scott Peck, *The Road Less Traveled* (New York: Simon & Schuster, 1978) 40.

[4]*The Mission*, prod. Fernando Ghia, dir. Roland Jaffé, 1986, Warner Bros.

[5]Paul Tillich, "The Truth Shall Make You Free," *Twenty Centuries of Great Preaching*, ed. Clyde E. Fant, Jr., and William M. Pinson, Jr., Vol. 10 (Waco: Word, 1971) 72.

[6]William E. Hull, *John*, Broadman Bible Commentary, ed. Clifton J. Allen, Vol. 9 (Nashville: Broadman Press, 1970) 73.

[7]Tillich, 73.

[8]Miller.

2.
Journey Without Map

Ruth 1, 2, 4:13-17

Lynda Weaver-Williams

(After leading Northminster Church in a weekend study of the Old Testament book of Ruth, sometimes teaching while members of the congregation were making bread, Lynda Weaver-Williams spoke directly to Northminster's pilgrimage on Sunday morning, 6 October 1991. She is an adjunct professor at Virginia Commonwealth University in Richmond.)

A young woman was giving a tour to French visitors in Washington: museums, monuments, you know the circuit. At the end of the day one of the French men asked, "But where are your saints?" In his country, statues of saints were on every corner: Saint Joan, Saint Cecilia, Saint Louis, Saint Bernadette. So he wondered, "Where are your saints?"

If someone were to ask us that question, we could answer with the story before us today. Where are our saints? Right here: Ruth, Naomi, Boaz. Now, we have no statues, but we do have a living story of very real people who know grace and show grace to one another, even in the midst of very hard times. They are our saints, all the more valued because they are so human. Hear now the exquisite story of Ruth, Naomi, and Boaz.

"Life is completely unfair; it breaks everybody's heart." So goes a line from a television play called *The Last Convertible*. Sooner or later life is completely unfair and everybody's heart gets broken. This story is all about broken hearts, broken dreams, and broken lives. The writer spares us not one sentimental tear or "once upon a time" beginning. This story begins with the breaking of a family from its roots.

A very severe famine caused at least one family to leave. The situation had to be difficult for this Jewish family to leave its God-given land and travel to a foreign place, but the members packed and left in search of food.

Then the tragedies began to multiply; in this foreign land of Moab—far from family and friends—Elimelech, the father and husband, died, leaving the widow Naomi to raise two sons on her own. In time, the sons married, but they took Moabite wives. They married outside of their faith, yet another sorrow for Naomi.

Then, when you think this woman had all she could take, her sons died and left no heirs. Barrenness in the family matched the barreness of the land the family left. There were broken hearts and empty arms all around—a circle of tragedies—and in the center stood Ruth, Naomi, and Orpah.

Bishop Tutu of South Africa said that when we meet the Almighty, God will ask only one question: "Where are your wounds?" Where are your wounds? This is a fair question, considering the source.

Naomi, Orpah, and Ruth had a fair answer: three funerals in five verses and still no cradle to rock; here are our wounds. These women had learned to enter into what the poet calls the "common weeping of the world."[1] Their wounds were their admission tickets to the world's suffering.

In many black churches today, some special women sit near the front of the sanctuary. Sometimes they even dress in white as if they are nurses. These women are caretakers. They have been charged with the well-being of the congregation each Sunday morning during worship. Their job is to enter the common weeping of the world that is expected to break forth as the Spirit moves in people's hearts.

Now, these women might come up beside you and offer you a tissue because one of them has noted that your tears are flowing. One of them might stand beside you, offering a steady shoulder to lean on as hymns are sung and prayers are offered. One of them might lay hands of blessing on you as she walks by. The role of these women is to comfort and caress, offer arms of support, and enter the common weeping of the world.

We too are called to the suffering places where everybody's hearts are broken. The story of Ruth, Orpah, and Naomi reminds us that in the suffering places we meet God. You know these places, the suffering places: the hospital room of an AIDS patient, the waiting room of any welfare clinic, the barred rooms of the city jail, the empty rooms of a widower's home, the glass rooms where crack-addicted babies are cradled, the soup kitchen room, the emergency room, rooms of the abused women's shelter, or any room where people suffer. These are the places we are called to be; and if we find ourselves in these rooms, we will find ourselves companions to God.

We leave Ruth and Naomi as they moved heavy-footed and slowly up the path toward Bethlehem. As they climbed, Naomi voiced her lament to God. She answered where her wounds were: here and here and here. She cried out against the bitterness of her life.

The last word of the chapter is not lament; God's last word is never despair. Naomi returned to Bethlehem, her home, at harvest time when there was at least the hint of fullness. She did not go alone; her companion every step of the way was a woman of promise. God's last word is never despair. God's last word is always hope.

A famous painting of this story hangs in many Sunday School rooms. It depicts Ruth in the fields, with sickle in hand. As the sun drops low behind her, the young woman with a kerchief around her head—who looks for all the world like a French peasant—stops and lifts her face toward the sky. The name of the painting is not "Ruth Gleaning" or "The Barley Harvest," but "The Song of the Lark."

"The Song of the Lark"? You have to wonder, what does this title have to do with Ruth? She was a remarkable young woman who, it seems, could hear things others could not—perhaps the song of a bird, even in the heat of harvest work. It seems she heard something else that led her from her home in Moab to Bethlehem.

In chapter two of Ruth, we are reminded three times in twenty-three verses that Ruth was a Moabitess, which we already know from several references in chapter one. She was a foreigner, the storyteller seems to underline. Yet she made a radical declaration of faith to Yahweh: She told Naomi, "Your God (shall be) my God" (1:16). She claimed allegiance to the one true God and thereby cut ties to home, family, friends, and previous faith to prove it.

Rarely in scripture do such declarations come unaided. Abraham and Sarah needed several divine visitations and promises to convince them to leave. With Noah, at least the voice of God spoke and got him moving toward the hardware store for ark instructions, and Moses needed God to present a burning bush as a calling card so that he would believe.

Ruth, the Moabitess, with no call or promise, chose Israel's God as her own. Yet, this choice was not the biggest surprise in the story. Rather, before Ruth chose Yahweh—the God of Israel—Yahweh chose Ruth —a foreign woman—as a part of the plan of redemption. We cannot forget that Ruth became the great grandmother of King David, who was the great, great, great, great grandparent of Jesus. Remember, she was a foreigner.

Can you not hear the gossip? "Why, she's not our kind. Just what is she doing here with Naomi, anyway? She says she wants to be part of us and even to worship our God. Well, just maybe we don't want to share our God with the likes of her. She has her own ways, her own people; she can just go on back to her religion. We don't take kindly to strangers, even if they are part of God's plan." Yet Ruth stayed; she worked in the fields, gained the notice and protection of Boaz, and all the while kept her pledge in the background: "Your God shall be my God."

God's plans always have larger dimensions than ours. We are always looking for ways to leave people out: Who can we not invite? In this story, it is clear God is looking for ways to gather people in, all the people.

Yahweh chose Ruth, and then it was only a matter of time. Naomi planned a midnight meeting, Ruth improvised at the threshing floor, and Boaz gallantly promised to do the right thing and redeem her as his bride —if the nearer kinsman yielded. Once again God's purposes were served through unlikely saints: a grief-stricken old woman who already had given up on everything; an old man as generous with his barley as his blessing; and Ruth, the Moabitess, with lots of initiative but the wrong bloodlines. It did not matter; Yahweh chose her anyway.

What might this mean? God's truth is enacted here by a woman, a minority woman. Perhaps the messenger is as important as the message. Perhaps we might be on the lookout for truth in a similarly unexpected persons. Maybe truth is to be discovered in the wrong bloodlines, revealed in the foreign face (or does that face just seem foreign?). Just maybe God's truth might even be hidden among us.

This story is read traditionally during the Feast of Weeks when the harvest is celebrated; when there is a sense of extravagance; when there is abundant cause to know that once again, God has provided more than enough. We read this story at the time of harvest as well; and we are reminded of God's abundant presence among us and the extravagance of grace in Christ Jesus. We are reminded that once again God has provided more than enough forgiveness.

We read this story and remember that God is still interested in harvests: God is still busy about gathering people in—the ones we leave out and forget, the ones we do not like. God is still gathering. Like the dropped sheaves of grain, God is yet gathering up the forgotten and left-behind ones and bringing all creation together in a great and glad harvest. Hear now the happy ending of the story.

My friend Anne Neil, missionary of many years to Africa, calls this story "journey without map." Ruth and Naomi traveled together not knowing what their journey would hold or where it would take them. Naomi spent time being angry at God; they both spent time wondering where the next meal was coming from. Yet they traveled.

Two together, and then three with Boaz joining them, and then four with the newborn baby—none of them knew that the journey of their family would lead to royalty, that Israel's greatest king would claim them as ancestors. They simply traveled on, and the child's laughter was reminder enough that whatever was before them, God had already been unbelievably good.

Naomi's empty arms were full with a child; the widow Ruth became a wife; a family's name was not only restored, but elevated. These are indeed our kind of saints: extraordinary people living ordinary lives. In this story God's ways were made known not through earthquakes and pillars of fire, but through simple kindnesses, unexpected courage, radical promises, and through what David Buttrick calls "the high courtesies of love."

The family of Bethlehem is a sign to us of another family that would walk the roads of Bethlehem, years later, carrying in their arms too a child of great promise. Ruth and Boaz were forerunners of another extraordinary man and woman named Mary and Joseph through whose ordinary lives God cared enough to give the very best.

Look around you. Among us right now, sitting next to you, are extraordinary people living ordinary lives of grace, kindness, and courage. Already God has been unbelievably good; that is part of why we are here, right? If there are such things as saints, these are our kind, right here sharing pews with us—extraordinary people living ordinary lives.

This "journey without map" has migrated from famine to fullness, barrenness to birth, and alienation to reunion. It is our story. As the Church, we move like Naomi and Ruth on a journey without map. We pass through famine times and full times, too; we live among broken hearts and birthing rooms; we know what it is like to be strangers living in a strange culture, for we are the Church, always on the move so as to keep track of our Holy Guide.

So we move on, maybe without a map, but not without companions. As you set out on your travels, looking for what new might come to you at this point of beginning again, may Ruth and Naomi speak to you of courage and kindness and of the God of the Harvest—the arms full, wide open harvest that even includes those forgotten and left behind—for such is the kingdom of God.

Endnotes

[1]Miguel Unamuno, *The Tragic Sense of Life*, 17.

II.
Becoming

"Now you . . . are children of the promise."
(Gal 4:28)

"You stand assembled today all of you, before the Lord your God . . . to enter into the covenant of the Lord your God, . . . which the Lord your God is making with you this day; . . . that he may establish you today as his people, and that he may be your God, as he promised you."

(Deut 29:12-13)

"Contend for the faith that was once for all entrusted to the saints."
(Jude 3)

"We are a church!" After only three weeks, this was the conviction of the small group of people who had been meeting for worship in the living room of Kay Southern's house. No one knew whether or not "the church" would last. No one even knew for sure where being "a church" would lead the group. The thirty-five or forty people, who less than one month earlier had felt like nobodies without a church, however, were absolutely convinced that they had become—or were becoming—a church.

Before the calendar year of 1988 ended, these folks declared to the public what they had already confessed among themselves: "We are a church!" Members of the congregation excitedly invited friends not involved in another local church to join them for worship. Appropriate legal papers were filed to form a corporation to be known as "The Monroe Church."

The small band of believers that had gathered just prior to Thanksgiving Day to discuss with each other and to lay before God their shock, hurts, fears, anxieties, and faint hopes was not out of the wilderness yet, but these people were moving—together. They approached Christmas Day with strong hopes, mounting courage, and a readiness to allow the love of God to become flesh again in them. A new church had been born.

Developments were occurring at a speed far greater than anyone had dared anticipate. Not everyone was moving so rapidly, though. Ralph Webb, who had continued to think of returning to his former church, remembers that "It was scary." Dibble Pate actually protested what was happening: "I am too old" to start a new church. Similarly, Harold Hughens said that he did not have the physical and emotional energy required for such a mission.

Then, these very individuals and others like them began to change their minds as rapidly as their friends forged ahead. Ralph Webb said that once he took a good look at the people involved, he felt it could really work—that a church could be born. Dibble Pate indicated that the realization "We're together" moved her along quickly and happily. Harold Hughens confessed with a smile that after worrying that he did not have the strength needed to be a part of a new church, he had never in his life felt as energized as he did working in this rapidly emerging fellowship.

Making Decisions

Less than two months after the initial gathering for talk and worship, a small but excited and energetic group of people was busy at work on a new church. Almost immediately questions of structure and organization had to be answered, questions many people in the group did not want raised. These reticent members had watched local churches structure the life right out of their fellowships, developing a devotion to organization that actually hampered the church's mission.

The necessity of decision-making generated a sizable amount of anxiety. Many of these people had grave problems with the traditional methods of decision-making they had experienced in other churches. They adamantly opposed a few individuals (whether officially or informally) making choices and establishing policies that affected everybody. From its inception, this new fellowship had given every appearance of being different—intentionally different in its approach to public worship and its acceptance of religious castaways—from what its members had known before. But, would that be the case as, for the first time, important decisions had to be made about the church's identity, governance, and ministry?

Taking a Name

Ralph and Priscilla Asbury hosted a series of luncheon meetings for the church's membership to discuss a name for the church and consider the denominational and other organizational groups with which the church would affiliate. An indication of things to come rapidly appeared in these sessions. Everybody had an opinion and freely expressed it, as the members desired. The congregation was unyielding in its resolve that whatever had to be done, it would do as a family—a family of faith.

Considerations of a name for the church prompted deliberations on the congregation's denominational identity. Some folks, like Bill Krutzer, offered a substantial rationale for not incorporating the word "Baptist" in the church's name. Others, like Nellen Hughens, voiced strong feelings in support of claiming a Baptist identity by way of the church's name. After a full, no-holds-barred discussion of this issue, the congregation decided to vote on it and abide by the results of the vote.

At this point, the sensitivity, respect, and care for each other that have so uniquely characterized this group of people throughout their pilgrimage took over. By means of a written vote, a decision was made not to use the word "Baptist" in naming the church. Dominant reasons for this action included a desire to be open to all people and a concern that the word "Baptist" in the church's name would cause many people to stereotype the congregation inaccurately. The democratic process had worked, and a majority point of view had been established. The vote was close, however, and the voters' goal was to be a church. D. H. Clark suggested that the word "Baptist" be included in the congregation's legal corporate name though not in its title. Everyone supported this idea.

What a great compromise! This act further strengthened the fellowship. It also convinced Jim and Joyce Files, who had been visiting in the congregation, that this was the kind of family of faith in which they should be involved—a fellowship in which people respect each other even when they disagree with each other, a body of believers disinterested in the categories of winners and losers.

Choosing a name for the church was a much easier decision than the prior one on denominational affiliation. Out of numerous suggestions, two proposals quickly surfaced as the most popular: Northminster Church and Christ Church. After a full discussion of each possibility, a vote was taken, and the name "Northminster Church" won by a large margin. This rapidly evolving congregation of people, most of whom lived on the north side of town at the time of this vote, eagerly identified itself as a fellowship of God's people open to everybody and committed to ministry.

Appointing Leaders

Throughout their brief life together, all members of the Northminster fellowship had been involved in everything the fellowship did—making logistical preparations for meetings, discussing decisions that had to be made, participating in every aspect of corporate worship experiences, and planning ministries. Virtually every individual, children and teenagers included, had assumed a responsibility and carried it out faithfully. Never before had "doing church" been such a totally participatory endeavor. And, it was fun. Absolutely no one wanted to lose the spirit of family that had emerged from such broad-based involvement in the church,

though everybody recognized a growing need for a leadership mechanism
of some kind.

Again, people held their breaths, hoping that the newness and fulfill-
ment of what they were finding together would not be destroyed by old
patterns of organization. Distrust among the members of Northminster
was not a problem, but almost everyone in the fellowship harbored a bad
memory of abuses of church leadership somewhere in their past. Too
much was at stake for a mistake to ruin it.

During one of their lunch meetings in the Asbury's home, Northminster members decided to appoint a coordinating committee that would
discuss issues related to the church's life and then bring recommendations on these issues to the whole church. Most everyone seemed
satisfied with the non-threatening idea of a "coordinating" group. By a
vote of the congregation, four persons were named to serve as the first
coordinating committee: Priscilla Asbury, Harold Hughens, Kay Southern,
and Craig Henry. The church expressed its will that a gender balance always be maintained in this body.

Counting Coins and Pondering Missions

Shortly after its organization, Northminster Church had no indebtedness
or a budget. Members of the fellowship gave their tithes and offerings
through the body incorporated as "The Monroe Church." Some people instructed Connie Smallwood, who volunteered to serve as the church's
treasurer, to forward a part of their financial contributions to the Southern
Baptist Alliance (an organization that later changed its name to the Alliance of Baptists).

The church needed a budget. No one, however, had any idea of the
amount of income the church could anticipate. Finally, after sharing a
meal together, all participants in the fellowship were requested to write
down on a sheet of paper the amount of money they planned to give to
the church for the remainder of the year. Those figures were totaled, and
Northminster Church projected a first year's income of $90,000.

Decisions had to be made about expenditures. Contemplating these
decisions, members of the congregation once again raised questions about
the church's affiliations. Divergent opinions appeared. A congregational
meeting convened for the purpose of allowing everyone to participate in
a thorough discussion of the church's financial mission.

On 2 April 1989, the congregation adopted a budget that provided for guest worship leaders, worship resources, educational materials, expenses related to a meeting place, and missions involvements through other religious groupings. Eventually this latter category was defined more specifically and funds were allocated to the local Baptist association, the Louisiana Baptist Convention, the Southern Baptist Convention, and the Southern Baptist Alliance.

Employing Ministers

Also included in Northminster Church's first budget was a salary for a part-time minister of the arts. A month later, the four-member coordinating committee of the church made a specific recommendation that the title of this position be changed to associate pastor and minister of the arts, and that Don Nixon be called by the church to do this ministry on a full-time basis. Additionally, the committee recommended that the church call Cathe Nixon to function part time as the director of educational ministries.

Most of the people in the Northminster fellowship had grown to love the Nixons and marvel at their expertise in ministry while together in another church in Monroe. They had been surprised, but pleased, when Don and Cathe chose to identify with their emerging church and function faithfully as volunteer ministers within it. Thus, words from the coordinating committee's letter of recommendation to the church resonated positively with the convictions of the membership: "At this time in the life of our church, we strongly believe that Don is the ideal person to provide necessary leadership in the area of pastoral care as well as to lead us in the area of music and the other arts. . . . Cathe can bring much needed focus and direction to our Christian education program for all ages, and especially for our children and youth."

With the adoption of its coordinating committee's recommendations a few weeks later, Northminster Church took another giant leap of faith that almost immediately proved invaluable in strengthening its redemptive presence in Monroe. Both Don and Cathe were superbly trained, uniquely skilled, and highly motivated individuals with a gift for creativity, a biblical vision of the meaning of real church, and a commitment to hard work. With profound gratitude for the opportunity to serve in this kind

of church, the Nixons began to give themselves completely to the work
of this body of believers.

Some folks in Northminster Church feel strongly that the church
might not have continued had not Don Nixon been present among them
and accepted their call to minister there. That sentiment probably reflects
the depth of their love and appreciation for Don and Cathe more than an
accurate reading of the situation. All indications are that God was at
work bringing a new congregation into existence, and that "the gates of
hell would not prevail against it." Without a doubt, though, the church
would not have learned the dynamics of caring, developed such excellence in its experiences of worship, and impacted the community so
powerfully as quickly as it did had Don Nixon not been its minister.

Making a Covenant

Several people in the new church pushed for the formal adoption of a
covenant, a church covenant that would serve as a core statement of the
congregation's identity and commitments. Only one serious reservation
about a covenant surfaced: Keep it simple. No opposition to the adoption
of a covenant appeared.

Knowing that various members of the congregation had been appreciatively involved in the Southern Baptist Alliance since its inception,
Priscilla Asbury suggested that the church consider adopting a form of
the covenant embraced by that national organization. Members of Northminster's coordinating committee concurred and offered Priscilla's
suggestion as a recommendation, which other members of the church en-
thusiastically accepted in a business meeting.

On Palm Sunday, 19 March 1989, in the great room of D. H. and
Hannah Clark's house—a room strewn with greenery and filled with a
spirit of festivity—the congregation of Northminster Church looked back
to the Christ behind them, repeating the ancient shout, "Hosanna to the
Son of David," and looked ahead to the Christ going before them.
Eighty-eight members signed the church's charter and recited the
church's covenant. All three acts of devotion to Christ thrust this new
expression of the body of Christ further into its own experience of crucifixion and resurrection.

Acknowledging that "The grace of God is making of us a fellowship
to embody and express the Spirit of Christ," members of the

Northminster fellowship covenanted "to love God with all our heart, mind, soul, and strength" and vowed "to love each other as we love ourselves." Covenanters pledged support for

> the freedom of the local church, under the authority of Jesus Christ to shape its own life and mission, call its own leadership, and ordain whom it perceives as gifted for ministry, male or female.

From the first moment of their corporate life, the people in this fellowship demonstrated an inflexible resolve to function as a servant community in relation to the world and as a supportive communion in relation to all other Christians. Not surprisingly, then, both dimensions of this resolve found expression in the church's covenant:

> We further commit ourselves to . . . the larger body of Jesus Christ, expressed in various Christian traditions, and to cooperation with believers everywhere in giving full expression to the Gospel . . . (to) the servant role of leadership within the church, following the model of our Servant Lord, and to full partnership of all God's people in mission and ministry.

What happened? And, how? From amid a small group of aimless, hurting people, an exciting, intentional community of faith was born. Individuals who had entered Advent desperately searching for direction and hope arrived at Palm Sunday, only weeks later, brimming with hope and sprinting toward the "high calling of Christ."

How does one explain what happened? Good-natured friends have said laughingly that they expected nothing less from this workaholic band of type A personalities. More seriously, though, these same friends of members of the congregation admit that even they were surprised by the rapid emergence and instantaneous impact of this community of faith.

In reality, the public expression of church that took form so quickly among this small group of people had a long period of gestation privately. In a sense, these folks were well on their way to becoming a new church months, if not years, before they ever scheduled their first gathering.

Ernestine Westbrook acknowledges that the people in this new fellowship had thoughts about the meaning of church that differed dramatically from prevailing views in the congregations from which they came. For a long time, these folks had wrestled with a profound dissatisfaction related to budget priorities, educational goals, missions support, missions strategies, and a lack of openness to women in ministry in the other churches to which they belonged. Occasionally, when together in a social setting, they would talk about their concerns. Several participants in the new movement recall that years earlier, in one of many moments of frustration, Craig Henry had declared, "We need to start a new church!"

Please do not mistake my observation of what happened for an explanation of what happened. Sequentially chronicled events and carefully reasoned narratives cannot tell the whole story. An element of mystery unmistakably dominates this account. Dibble Pate voiced the reality: "We didn't take control; something took control of us!" God was in it. True to the biblical tradition, God was forming a new community of people out of a group of hurting, displaced people. In what could have been a time of disillusionment and tragedy, God inspired new visions and provided the visionaries with the courageous strength required to pursue them. As with ancient Israel, God entered a bad situation and turned it into an exciting new initiative in the cause of redemption.

The corporate worship experiences of Northminster Church faithfully reflect the congregation's pilgrimage. One of the people's most cherished litanies allows them to voice together one of their most profound convictions:

> We will tell our children:
> Once we were slave people
> And now we are free.
> Once we were no people
> And now we are God's people.

No one suspected that what happened among them was anything other than the work of God in their lives. Another line in this same litany makes that truth abundantly clear: "On that first morning God called us."

A contagious enthusiasm about the potential of Northminster Church could not erase from the members' minds the pain that prompted their pilgrimage and the anxieties that continued to accompany their adventure. Committed to honesty, the church knew that when its story was told—whether to the children in its midst or to others interested in its development—the whole story had to be told. So, in a litany of worship, members avowed,

> God called us from nothing. Out of nothing came being. . . . Out of chaos came order. Out of nothing came life. . . . This morning God calls us to be the people of faith in the midst of meaninglessness. . . . Out of brokenness God calls us to wholeness. Out of divisiveness God calls us to community. Out of tears God calls us to laughter. Out of self-centeredness God calls us to love one another. Out of unfaithfulness God calls us to faith.

Northminster Church embodies the gospel it proclaims, not only pointing to hope but incarnating hope.

> Out of death to resurrection,
> Out of chaos to birth,
> Out of unfaithfulness to faith.

Is this situation a unique one? Not by any means. What happened in Monroe, Louisiana, as a group of people became Northminster Church, can happen elsewhere—anywhere a fellowship of folks is able to break with the security of slavery and tolerate enough freedom to venture boldly in pursuit of the pioneering, redeeming leadership of God.

3.
The Church in the New Testament

Frank Stagg

(On 6–7 April 1990, Frank Stagg led members of Northminster Church in four hours of discussion regarding the nature of a New Testament Church. Dr. Stagg lives "Under the Live Oaks" in Diamondhead, Mississippi.)

The term "church," like the Scottish "Kirk" and German *Kirche*, is of uncertain origin; but it probably derives from the Greek adjective *kyriakos* (from *kyrios*, "Lord"), "of the Lord" or "belonging to the Lord." *Kyriakos* appears twice in the New Testament: for "the Lord's Supper" (1 Cor 11:20) and "the Lord's Day" (Rev 1:10). Probably by analogy, the term came to designate "the Lord's house" or "the Lord's people," i.e., the Church. So employed, the term preserves a basic New Testament claim; the Church is "God's Church" (1 Cor 1:2; 2 Cor 1:1), under the lordship of Christ. It is not "the Church" simply because it bears some name, or because it functions democratically and autonomously, or because it confesses certain doctrines. It is "the Church" only if it exists under the lordship of Jesus Christ. Jesus called it "my church" (Matt 16:18). If it is not his, it is not the Church.

Persons of whatever race, ethnic identity, or sex are called individually to Jesus as the Christ. Thus, a Christian's primary relationship is with Christ, not coerced but voluntary on each side. In this basic calling to Christ we also are "called into the *koinonia* (fellowship) of His (God's) Son, Jesus Christ, our Lord" (1 Cor 1:9). The "one loaf" and "one cup" attest to this oneness of all who are "in Christ" (1 Cor 10:16-17). Thus the church is a fellowship of persons responding to God's calling, made one people (in covenant) under Christ's lordship. Ecclesia is *koinonia* under the *basileia* (kingdom) of God's Anointed.

Ekklesia

The English word "church" usually translates the Greek *Ekklesia* (literally, "called out"). The full term is "the *ekklesia* of God" (Acts 20:28; 1 Cor 1:2; 10:32; 11:22; 15:9; 2 Cor 1:1; Gal 1:13; 1 Tim 3:5, 15) or "the churches of God" (1 Cor 11:16; 1 Thess 2:14; 2 Thess 1:4). The Church universal is the primary reality; a local church is "the Church" wherever persons are gathered under the lordship of Christ. The "autonomy" of a local church derives from this reality.

The term *ekklesia* was widely used in the Greek-speaking world in New Testament times for a local assembly called out by a town crier; but it is a serious mistake to understand New Testament usage simply by pagan usage. There are affinities and differences in usage. The New Testament sees Christians as people of divine "calling," hence "called out." Christians also appear in local assemblies, but *ekklesia* is not limited to local usage in the New Testament. There is but one Church universally (ecumenical), and this one Church appears wherever followers of Jesus Christ are gathered in his presence and under his lordship. The Church universal is not the sum of local churches; rather, a local church is derivative of the Church universal. It is "The Church" at Corinth, Thessalonica, Philippi, or wherever.

The local church is "autonomous" in that it is "the Church" wherever persons are gathered under the Lordship of Christ. Under Christ's authority, the local church may worship, preach, teach, or minister within its fellowship or beyond. A local church does not have to seek authority from a superior Church, for it lives directly under the lordship of Christ, the ultimate authority over the Church. The Church is not "autonomous" in the ultimate sense, for that authority belongs to Christ alone. By congregational (democratic) process, the Church at any level is to seek Christ's will and way. It is the Church only under the lordship of Christ, not by autonomy or democracy.

The non-local use of *ekklesia* appears variously in the New Testament. When Jesus declared that he would build his Church and that it would be indestructible (Matt 16:18), he was not speaking of any local church (they come and go). Acts 9:31 speaks of the Church universal, "the *ekklesia* throughout the whole of Judea, Galilee, and Samaria." Paul confessed to having persecuted "the *ekklesia* of God" (Gal 1:13; 1 Cor 15:9; see also Phil 3:6), seen here as one Church, not simply churches. In 1 Corinthians 10:32, the *ekklesia* is one of "three races," along with Jews and Greeks (here a synonym for Gentiles). The one Church is envisioned in 1 Corinthians 12:28 and Hebrews 12:22f. The oneness of the Church is necessarily the idea behind the model, "the Body of Christ."

The term *ekklesia* appears in only two verses in the four Gospels: for the Church universal (Matt 16:17) and for the local Church (Matt 18:17), which has been taken by some to imply that Jesus did not intend to build the Church. A noted scholar said, "Jesus proclaimed the Kingdom of God, but instead the Church appeared!" This confuses the question.

True, the term *ekklesia* appears only twice in the Gospels, but the idea is there under such terms and models as the Shepherd's flock (Mark 14:27 par; Luke 12:32; John 10:1-18; 21:15-17), the family (Mark 3:35), and the true vine (John 15:1-8). Yet more significant is Jesus' call to all persons who are willing to hear: "Follow me." Jesus did not just offer teaching and example; he called persons to himself and thus to one another to form a new people, however termed (cf Mark 2:14; 8:34; 10:21; Matthew 4:19; 8:22; 9:9; 11:28; 16:24; 19:21; Luke 5:27; 9:23, 59; 18:22; John 1:43; 10:27; 12:26; 21:22). He declared his family to consist of whoever does the will of God (Mark 3:33-35).

The Church and the Kingdom

The Church universal is not to be confused with the kingdom of God. The kingdom of God is the sovereign rule of God. God is King! God's kingship confronts us ultimately in Jesus the Christ. The Hebrew *Messiah* and Greek *Christos* (both terms for "anointed") designate God's "anointed," anointed to rule. Therefore, Jesus proclaimed, "The *kairos* (season) has been fulfilled, and the Kingdom of God has drawn near" (Mark 1:15).

Jesus rejected the view widely held in the Judaism of his time that the Messiah would defeat the enemies [of the Jewish people] and "restore the kingdom to Israel" (See Acts 1:6, where even the post-Resurrection disciples cling to this idea). Three wars were fought between the Jews and Romans (A.D. 66–73; 115–117; 132–135), with messianic expectations that God would give victory over the Romans. The General of the Jewish armies in the war of A.D. 132-135 (known as *Bar Cocheba*) was hailed by Rabbi Akiba as "Messiah." The Dead Sea Scroll, "The War Between the Sons of Light and the Sons of Darkness," in its dramatic form holds to this confidence. Jesus rejected this view of the Kingdom of God, from his wilderness temptations to Golgotha and emphatically when he rebuked Peter at Caesarea of Philippi (Mark 8:27–9:1).

Peter correctly confessed Jesus to be "the Christ," but he was stubbornly wrong when he rejected what Jesus said about his coming rejection and death (8:31-33). Jesus established the kingdom of God with a cross, not a sword, and by giving his life and not taking life. He made this, his way, the basis for discipleship (8:34-38).

The Body of Christ

Paul saw the Church as "the Body of Christ." He never speaks of "a body of Christians." He saw Christ not as dead but alive, not absent but present, not emeritus but active, continuing his ministry not in a ghostly form but embodied in his followers—the Church, in a real sense Christ's own body. Of course, this is an analogy, not to be taken in a crudely literal sense, but to be taken seriously. In a real sense, his followers are *his body* as they are his temple (1 Cor 3:16; Eph 2:21).

Paul employed the analogy of the body in several letters, each time elucidating the nature and function of the Church. He clarified the matter of "spiritual gifts," so abused in Corinth (1 Cor 12) by showing that the various gifts in the Church are not to be competitive or occasions for boasting. This reference is his first traceable employment of the analogy of the body for the Church. Paul showed that a body is comprised of many members, yet is one body and concluded, "Thus is Christ" (12:12). We may have expected, "Thus is the Church." The Church is one body with many members, but is Christ's body!

Seeking to overcome divisions within the church at Corinth, Paul pled that no member of the body is to be compared unfavorably with another member. Just as we do not compare "apples and oranges," so each member of the body is to be respected in terms of its proper function. So in the Church! Paul dared to declare, "By one Spirit we all were baptized into one body," whatever our differences by nature or circumstance (12:13). Such distinctions as Jew or Greek, bond or free, male or female are irrelevant to being "in Christ"—whether as to salvation, ministry, or whatever (Gal 3:27-28).

Paul returned to the analogy of the body in Romans 12:3-8. Again he warned against conceit over what actually are gifts, differing in the Church as in a body. Again he stressed the fact that a body is necessarily a unity as well as a plurality of members, each member differing from the others.

Gifts within the Church as the Body of Christ are indeed gifts, so to be received in gratitude and not in pride. Paul stressed not only the variety of gifts, but the fact that the possession of a gift obligates its exercise. His term for "gifts" is *charismata*, the plural for *charisma* (any gift of *charis,* which means "grace"). He made a play on words, "*charismata* according to *charin.*" These are "charismatic gifts."

All gifts are "charismatic," or gifts of grace. These include "eternal life" (Rom 6:23) and such gifts as listed in Romans 12:6-8. Stewardship and administration are listed with preaching and teaching as charismatic!

This passage compels a reassessment of the role of those called "laypersons," men and women. In fact, it undercuts our distinctions between "clergy" and "laity"; for the possession of a gift obligates one to its exercise. Not all "God's chullen got shoes," but all of God's children have gifts (*charismata*). As in Galatians 3:27-28, "in Christ" there is "not any Jew or Greek, not any slave or free, not any male and female," all being "one in Christ Jesus"; so in Romans 12:6-8, such distinctions are irrelevant to those possessing gifts of God's grace. It is a wrong question to ask if "laypersons," men or women, have the "right" to pulpit or pastoral ministry. The right question asks, "Do they have the right not to minister in terms of whatever gifts they have?"

Both Colossians and Ephesians build heavily on the analogy of the Church as the body of Christ. In Colossians, Paul's focus is christological, where Christ is "the head of the body, that is the Church" (1:18). Christ's sufferings continue in those who suffer "in behalf of his body, which is the Church" (1:24).

In Ephesians, the central theme is the Church as the body of Christ. God has given Christ "head over all things to the Church, which is his body" (1:22f).

Ephesians 2:14-22 is classic! Here God's eternal plan for uniting the human family is declared. Christ is our peace, having broken down the "separating wall" between Jew and Gentile. This seemingly echoes Paul's being evicted from the Temple in Jerusalem on the charge of having taken a Gentile beyond the wall separating the uncircumcised from the circumcised (Acts 21:27-30). God has created "one fresh (*kainon*, not *neon*) kind of humanity," thus making peace! The terms "Church" and "body of Christ" are not explicit here, but the idea is present, along with other analogies ("fellow citizens of the saints," "members of the household of God," "a holy temple in the Lord," "a dwelling place of God in the Spirit").

Ephesians 4:11-16 is another classic, describing the ministry of the Church in terms of its Minister and ministers. Christ himself is *the Minister*. He continues his ministry in his Body, the Church. What we now call "equipping ministers" are given to the Church: "apostles, prophets, evangelists, and pastors and teachers." The list is not exhaustive, and no two such listings in the New Testament are identical. The living Christ gives to the Church these ministers "for the equipping of the saints for the work of ministry, unto the building up of the body of Christ" (4:12). It is not Christian ministry unless the living Christ is behind it and in it.

Ministry is not the function of some alone in the Church. All the "saints" (the New Testament's term for all followers of Jesus) are called to ministry, although they have different gifts and thus different ministries. Again, such distinctions as "clergy" and "laity" are undercut by this passage; and no distinction in ministry is made for men and women.

The Church and Its Structures

Jesus created the Church, but he did not organize it. He called persons to himself and thus to one another. Building on foundations already laid in his Jewish heritage, Jesus reconstituted "the people of God," known variously as his flock, family, temple, a holy nation, Church, Body of Christ, and otherwise.

Jesus appointed twelve apostles, possibly modeled on the twelve patriarchs. Their primary role was to bear witness to his life and ministry, from his baptism to his resurrection. (These apostles would have no successors, because no eyewitnesses would be alive after the first generation.) Jesus did institute a supper, with loaf and cup symbolizing his body and blood, both given in sacrificial service. Jewish elders are mentioned in the Gospels; but there is no trace of bishops, elders in a Christian sense, or orders otherwise in the Gospels. There were no "deacons" in the modern sense, the term *diakonos* designating anyone who serves in whatever way. Church structures, such as the Seven in Acts 6:1-6, appeared later, developed to meet needs as they arose.

Structures have a proper place in the Church to the extent that they serve in the ministries of the Church. They are like the "wineskins" in

Jesus' parable, subject to becoming brittle and leaky and needing to be replaced when they are no longer serviceable (Mark 2:22).

"Institutionalism" is the confusion of "wineskins" with "wine," making structures ends in themselves. In the intention of Jesus' parable, the "wine" is to be preserved at all costs; the "wineskins" do not exist for themselves and are dispensable or replaceable. To make "wineskins" an end in themselves is a form of idolatry.

The essence of the Church is Christ and his people, they living under his lordship and seeking to understand and follow his example, teaching, and way. Orders, structures, rituals, and confessions of faith are "wineskins," often serviceable but never ultimate.

Church Polity

The "polity" inherent in the Church is the lordship of Christ. Beyond this, the roots of various current polities are traceable in the New Testament. The Gospels have the least traces of church polity, although Matthew 18:17 implies a congregational polity, at least in discipline (so also 2 Cor 2:6). Paul claimed certain authority as an apostle, yet he had to plead with churches, as at Corinth, to comply with his leadership. Churches sometimes rejected his guidance. Bishops (overseers), elders (presbyters), and pastors (shepherds) interchange in Acts 20:17, 28; and elders and bishops interchange in Titus 1:5, 7. Shepherd and Overseer interchange in 1 Peter 2:25. It seems that from this early fluidity there emerged such orders as bishops, elders, and deacons.

The earliest Christians were Jews, and for some time they worshiped in synagogues and the Temple in Jerusalem. The synagogues were governed by laypersons, with a major focus on worship, preaching, teaching, and discipline. No priestly ministry was required for the synagogues.

The Temple was highly structured: high priest, lower priests, and Levites, with a focus on cultic rites and sacrifices. Ministry in the Temple was priestly. "Laypersons," such as Jesus and Paul, could enter the Court of Jewish Men but not the Holy Place or the Holy of Holies. Jewish women could not go beyond the Court of the Women. Gentiles were restricted to an outer court.

The Church in its varieties has drawn from both synagogue and Temple. Those more "word" oriented draw heavily from the synagogue. Those oriented toward rituals (thus priestly) draw heavily from the Temple.

Church Agenda

Worship, proclamation, study, discipline, evangelism, missions, care for needy people, and anything that serves the glory of God or the good of humanity belongs to the proper agenda of the Church. Guidance for developing the agenda of a Church may be found in such passages as Luke 4:16-30; 7:18-23; Matthew 25:31-46; 28:16-20; and throughout the New Testament in examples and specific teachings.

Human need itself goes far in setting the Church's agenda: individual emptiness calling for meaning; alienation calling for reconciliation; poverty calling for food, medical care, dignity, education, and more; abuses of power (money, military, political, and religious) calling for harnessing power for human good; and care for God's good creation, our larger "house" (the "eco" in "ecology" and "economy" is from the Greek *oikos*, which means house).

Primarily the Church is *to be the Church*! In the New Testament, *being* has priority over *doing* and *saying*. The Church is *to be* the *koinonia* of the Spirit. Ministry is not an option; it is inherent in salvation (Mark 8:34-38; 10:43-45; John 12:24-26). Just as the essence of being lost is to be self-serving, the essence of salvation is to be self-giving. Hence, ministry is inherent in salvation, not an option beyond salvation. This holds equally for women and men.

The Church is a covenant of persons under the lordship of Christ. It is a worshiping community, a witnessing community, and a caring community—beginning within itself. It is a prophetic community, seeking to hear the continuing Word of God and proclaiming it to itself and to the world, including the power structures of the world. Patriotism has its place, but religion that serves as public relations for the State is civil religion, with State in its pantheon of gods.

4.

Our Vocation: The Ministry of Reconciliation

2 Corinthians 5:14-21

Frank Stagg

(On Palm Sunday, 8 April 1990, Northminster Church renewed its covenant and dedicated the first piece of property it purchased. Frank Stagg preached this sermon following a weekend-long discussion of New Testament teachings on the nature of the church.)

The unit serving as our text is a golden nugget embedded in a letter composed of strata so varied that what we know as "Second Corinthians" may actually be a composite, pieced together from two or more letters from Paul to the church in Corinth. Our New Testament contains two letters known as First and Second Corinthians; but these two letters refer to at least two other letters, either completely lost or surviving partially as fragments put together in what we know as "Second Corinthians."

Paul said, "I wrote you in my letter not to be mixed up with fornicators" (1 Cor 5:9). He then corrected their misunderstanding of that letter; so clearly there was a letter prior to our "First Corinthians." 2 Corinthians 6:14–7:1 possibly may be a fragment of that lost letter. This unit is on the very subject of the lost letter and breaks the continuity between 2 Corinthians 6:13 and 7:2ff.

In 2 Corinthians 2:4 and 7:8-12 are references to yet another lost letter, described by Paul as so painful that he regretted writing it until he learned from Titus that it had borne fruit of reconciliation. Chapters 10–13 of our "Second Corinthians" may be a substantial part of this "painful letter." If so, it explains why chapters 1–9 are so irenic, and chapters 10–13 are so hostile. Both are understandable if seen in reverse order, chapters 10–11 from the earlier "painful letter" and chapters 1–9 from a letter after the reconciliation within the church and also between Paul and the church.

Paul's letters probably were not published as a corpus until after his death. The compiler/editor of the published letters may have found our "First Corinthians" intact but only fragments of other letters written by

Paul to Corinth. Written on fragile papyrus, these letters could easily have become fragmented. The compiler/editor may have mistakenly reversed the order of our chapters 1–9 and 10–13.

If, indeed, Paul's letters at Corinth may have fallen into such disarray, later to be lovingly edited, this says much for both the breakdown within the church and between Paul and the church, as well as the subsequent reconciliation. Estrangements within the Christian community are not new; they were there from the beginning. Estrangements are fatal only when they are not followed by reconciliation.

If our "Second Corinthians" was, indeed, pieced together by loving hands, it attests to both estrangement and reconciliation. The letter that was "painful" even to Paul for a time may have fallen into disarray in a church that for a time even challenged Paul's apostleship (1 Cor 1:9; 2 Cor 11:13, 12:11f.). Happily, the church experienced healing, and Paul's letters were preserved—even if with some loss. Even when reconciliation and healing result, scars often remain.

Whatever the history of our "Second Corinthians," the book is composed of sections in striking contrasts of mood, some irenic and some almost bitter. The church at Corinth was once fragmented, boasting of its partisan champions: "I of Paul, I of Apollos, I of Cephas, I of Christ" (1 Cor 1:12). Underneath the church's divisions was its "I" trouble. The members were egocentric. It was as though Christ himself were divided (1:13); for in dividing the church, the body of Christ, they were dividing Christ.

Happily, out of this chaos in Corinth emerged a church that survived for centuries. From it we have a legacy of letters edited as two letters. Embedded in the highly composite "Second Corinthians" is our golden nugget on "Our Vocation: the Ministry of Reconciliation."

For several years a committee of five professors from four seminaries and divinity schools worked on our text: Walter Harrelson and Richard T. Mead of Vanderbilt University, Nashville; Fredrick W. Danker of Lutheran School of Theology, Chicago; Jack P. Lewis of Harding University Graduate School of Religion, Memphis; and I of The Southern Baptist Theological Seminary, Louisville. We worked as the Hermeneutics Project of the Faith and Order Commission of the World Council of Churches. Appointed in 1965, our findings were published two decades later.[1] This sermon owes much to that study project.

The basic ingredients for reconciliation are packed into our text: "the love of Christ," which is behind it all; the death for others, which occurred first in Christ and which is to be followed in us; the reversal of the egocentric principle in us of living for ourselves, transformed into the principle of the Cross, where one dies and lives for others; a new way of seeing other people because of a new way of seeing Christ; followers of Jesus as "a new creation," old things having passed away and new things having become; God's ministry of reconciliation, to become our ministry of reconciliation; what God was doing "in Christ" as the pattern for what we "in Christ" are to be doing. Just as "in Christ" God was reconciling the world to himself, so we "in Christ" are to be reconciling the world to God and to one another. Our vocation "in Christ," clearly then, is to be God's ambassadors to the world for reconciliation: to God, ourselves, and one another.

Some points call for sharpened focus. "The love of Christ" (v. 14) is deliberately ambiguous. The phrase can mean Christ's love for us or our love for him; both are required. "Love" as used here is deeper than emotion. It is a disposition to relate to another for that one's good, whatever the cost. This love is found first in Christ, a love that took him all the way to the cross. Such love is basic to our own salvation and resultant ministry of reconciliation. That Christ died for all does not mean that automatically all persons shared in his death. It made no difference for Judas, Pilate, and countless others. Our dying with him awaits our commitment to him, but our salvation and resultant ministry of reconciliation requires our entering his kind of death to self and life given to others.

Verse 16 is Paul's own interpretation of his conversion, as related in the book of Acts, when Paul went from blindness to having something like scales fall from his eyes (Acts 9:8-18). Paul declared that he no longer knew anyone "according to the flesh" (v. 16). He meant that he no longer evaluated people as he once did in terms of outward or secondary factors such as ethnic origin, circumcision or other cultic rites, keeping the letter of the law, and so on.

Once Paul had a new vision or understanding of Messiah, he was compelled to have a new vision of every human being. As a Pharisee, he once saw the expected Messiah as one who would "restore the kingdom to Israel" (Acts 1:6). To Paul, then, Messiah would defeat the enemies of Israel and give the kingdom to such Israelites who were faithful to the Mosaic law. When he met the risen Christ, all of this changed. His whole value system had to be radically revised, as he described it in Philippians 3:4-11. His former "gains" became losses, and his new values were those found in Christ. The inclusiveness of Christ compelled Paul to give up his exclusiveness, seeing that "in Christ there is not any Jew and Gentile, not any bond and free, not any male and female" (Gal 3:28).

Existence for Paul was so radically different "in Christ" that he could declare that if anyone is "in Christ," there is a "new creation." Further, "Old things have passed away, and new things have become." This new creation derives from God, who "in Christ" has reconciled us to himself and given to us the ministry of reconciliation. This perspective undercuts all the ancient man-made atonement theories, in which an angry or offended God awaits payment before God is willing to forgive sins and save sinners. This sees God as the active agent, not passive object in reconciliation.

The English word "atonement" appears only once in the King James Version of the New Testament: "But we also joy in God through our Lord Jesus Christ, by whom we have now received the atonement" (Rom 5:11). Here, "atonement" translates the Greek *katallage*, everywhere else in the New Testament rendered "reconciliation." In the King James Version, "atonement" means "at-one-mind" (the Latin *mens, mentis* gives us our English words "mentality" or "mind"). "Atonement" is God's work in Christ of making us of "one mind" with himself. The "mind of Christ" is described in Philippians 2:5-11, where Christ is seen as forfeiting his every right as he sought to save us from our self-destruction, giving his life in so doing.

Even in Romans 5:11, we are the ones who "receive atonement." The only atonement teaching in the New Testament is that God atones sinners! God at a cost as great as the Cross makes us "at-one-mind" with God. This is not only our salvation; it is our vocation. Our vocation in Christ as ministers of reconciliation is rooted in Christ; it is rooted in our own salvation. To be saved is to be saving. To be redeemed is to be redeeming. To be set at liberty is to be liberating. All who are in Christ—men and women, boys and girls—are ministers; and Christian ministry necessarily includes the ministry of reconciliation.

The basic claim in verse 19 may be read as a christological or incarnational statement, "God was in Christ." Probably it is to be read as a missiological or vocational statement: "In Christ, God was reconciling the world to himself." That is what "in Christ" God was doing; that is what we "in Christ" should be doing. The vocation of reconciliation is inherent in the relationship.

Like a diamond, reconciliation is many faceted. It means that we are to be reconciled to God. God is the agent in this, but even God cannot unilaterally effect our reconciliation. We must receive it from God's grace. Reconciliation means reconciliation with ourselves. We do relate to ourselves, and we can be in basic conflict with ourselves. There is no peace for us unless we are, "in Christ," at peace with ourselves. Reconciliation means reconciliation with other persons. Again, this cannot be imposed unilaterally. Our part is that it not have to await our openness to it.

In biblical teaching, reconciliation includes our being at peace with the natural world, God's own creation. Our ecological disaster reflects not only its worsening condition but our own estrangement or even hostility toward the universe of which we are a part. "In Christ" we are to be reconciled to God, self, others, and nature; and we are to be ministers of reconciliation on all of these fronts.

Endnote

[1]Jack P. Lewis, ed., *Interpreting 2 Corinthians 5:14-21, An Exercise in Hermeneutics* (Lewiston NY: Edwin Mellen Press, 1989).

5.
Three Eternal Questions
for the Church and Individual

Sarah Frances Anders

(On 8 February 1989, an ice storm made travel in Monroe virtually impossible. Most churches in town were closed. On this Sunday morning, however, a larger than usual group of worshipers gathered in the home of D. H. and Hannah Clark to worship God and hear a sermon by Sarah Frances Anders. Dr. Anders is Professor Emeritus of Sociology at Louisiana College in Pineville.)

You need not be a social scientist or religionist to know that I would not be mistaken for the typical Southern Baptist minister. My gender is not appropriate—nor my attire. My education is as good or better; some of my experiences would qualify me for the label. You could be wrong in your first impression, however, for you and I all probably meet the essential criteria of both the Old and New Testaments for the role of the minister. Actually the Quakers or "Friends" are more biblical when they say that all in the church fellowship are equally called and judged by our ministry . . . for ordination is ecclesiastical, not scriptural.

Three of the most significant eternal questions between God and man are found within the first fifty chapters of the Bible, but recur in differing forms throughout its pages. They apply to all of us equally, individually and collectively as the church, and we confront them in the first pages of our life chronicles. They are asked not because God does not already have the answers, but because we need to confront the answers.

The first question occurs in Genesis 3, after the first humans had misbehaved and defied one of God's first instructions. They heard God coming through time and space, asking, "Where are you?" Actually they were crouched down, discovering that hands could not cover the naked truth of dislocation from God's purpose. As persons and as a fellowship, you need to be perfectly clear about your location to God and God's plan for you.

The second question occurs in the next chapter when the offspring of this stumbling, experimenting couple were aware of brotherly differences and that they were not xerox copies of their parents. Cain was jealous because his manner of worship was not as pleasing to God as Abel's, and the first fratricide occurred. God queried him about the whereabouts of his brother. From that time to the present we have continued to commit fratricide by deed or neglect of our brothers and neighbors. We have answered, "You can't hold me responsible for the whereabouts and condition of my fellow humans." It is still as foolish an answer today as then.

The third question came after a long interview between God and Moses in a desert scene, with God calling him to deliver his people from bondage and Moses saying, "I just can't take on this job of rescuing my people." Ever since, we have been blind to our own gifts, equipment, and opportunities, hearing God say impatiently, "What on earth is that in your hand?" We do not see any connection between taking care of our own herd of sheep and delivering another one from dire troubles.

When I consider the question "Where are you?" I place myself in time. My adult decades have dipped over into the four most turbulent decades not only in American history but in human existence, not just in secular technology but in spiritual humanology, and not just in techniques of aggression but in patterns of human rights and otherness.

My place is not quite so expansive as my mother's. Her life dipped over into every decade of this twentieth century. As a child, she knew something of the first decade when immigrants flooded into our country almost a million per year, bringing phenomenal changes in factorization, urbanism, and family lifestyles. She was a teenager in the Terrible Teens of this century when America experienced her first global war, surviving perhaps the highest rates of drug abuse before or since, and she was old enough to vote in the first election open to women voters!

I heard her talk about the Roaring Twenties, followed by that great leveler of humanity—the Depression. But I can recall the Fractured Forties when a second global holocaust put women into the labor force, separated over three million families, and contributed to the highest divorce rate before or since.

Nevertheless, a baby boom began that lasted almost through the Fifties. I was very much the student during those years, but I remember the smoldering rebellion of many kinds of minorities, a rebellion that spilled over into the Violent Sixties. They were fighting being poor, being female, being black, being "poped," and being drafted into a morally questionable war. Some of us have shared those same adult decades, so we stand roughly in the same place.

Five years ago, John Naisbitt, in his book *Megatrends,*[1] said that the major trends of our last decade placed us all in an information-based, high-tech world. Humans have always lived in a world of words, but now the exploding sea of words can be stored in far greater reservoirs than our brains. Only a small minority of us have a handle on filling and channeling those reservoirs. We are drowning in information, but starved for knowledge and values. There is evidence the high school graduates of the Eighties are the first generation of youth who are less skilled than their parents were for their future. There is then no guarantee that this vast universe of data will make our lifestyle any more productive, satisfying, or ethical.

Nineteen hundred years before Naisbitt, another John wrote:

> When all things began, the Word already was. The Word dwelt with God, and what God was, the Word was. The Word, then, was with God at the beginning, and through him all things came to be; no single thing was created without him. All that came to be was alive with his life, and that life was the light of men. The light shines on in the dark, and the darkness has never mastered it. So the Word became flesh: he came to dwell among us and we saw his glory, . . . full of grace and truth. (John 1:1-5, 14 NEB)

Luke said, besides being good, he went around doing good and healing the oppressed and second-class citizens of the world.

If Christ the Word became flesh, and if Christ is in us, our flesh is full of the Word. He said,

> In very truth . . . you . . . will do what I am doing, . . . and will do greater things still because I am going to the Father. (John 14:12 NEB)

Jesus had thirty-three years to be and do the Word; you and I may have twice thirty-three plus ten to do the Word.

I am persuaded that hearing the Word is our liberation—and hearing is an ongoing experience. I do not hear the Word now as I did at age fifteen, or twenty-five, or thirty-five. Every year I try to read two or three books on the pilgrimages of well-known pace-setters who became liberated and left their mark on human history—persons such as Margaret Mead or Will Campbell or those who wrote the Abingdon series such as Martin Marty, Phyllis Tribble, and Harvey Cox.

I particularly identified with Cox in *Just As I Am* as he pinpointed those moments in his growing up that brought him increasing freedom: when he watched his grandmother's social and religious activism long before the women's liberation movement was a major force; when he freed his being Southern Baptist from any concern for his social status; when he stood at and crossed over the Berlin Wall; when he marched and was jailed alongside Martin Luther King, Jr., in Alabama; and when he lived among the Latin American third world liberationists, learning how to stand tall before totalitarian powers.[2] At each point, ever-enlarging circles of freedom opened in front of him for the doing of the Word. Every liberating experience provided a new arena of servanthood, a way to serve mankind.

I experienced similar "freeing" experiences as I shared the same three decades of adulthood with Cox. As a naive and sheltered nineteen-year-old, I worked in a flophouse mission in inner city Louisville, teaching street urchins and overcoming repulsions about dirt, profanity, vices, and promiscuity. I remember working with literacy programs for the Spanish people in Texas and Florida long before it was in vogue with Cambodians and Vietnamese. I recall refusing to toss out a planned home mission study book that was very explicit about Christians and race relations in the later 1950s; and of having my denominational writing blue-penciled beyond recognition because I spoke out clearly for human rights, civil liberty, and gender equality. I remember the 1960s when I got threats at my door, on the phone, and in the street because I worked against poverty and bigotry in Cenla. I remember when people, even denominational leaders, used jokes—not anger, threats, or blue pencils—about equal rights for women. I believe we are freed by the Gospel to serve those who were any one of those. I learned that my own anger and defensiveness could blunt my effectiveness spiritually, socially, and academically.

Do you recall the account in Luke 13:10-14? Jesus was teaching in the synagogue on the sabbath when he saw a woman who was bent over and unable to stand straight. She had been crippled for eighteen years. Jesus told her that her infirmity was gone, and she straightened up and praised God. The leader of the synagogue was angry.

David Owens, in *South of the Garden*, made an interesting observation on the words "spirit" and "infirm." To be infirm can mean to be weak, feeble, or diminished; while spirit can mean disposition, life force or even vivaciousness. To say that the bent-over woman was suffering an infirmed spirit suggests that her life force had deteriorated; she could no longer even be angry about her oppression. For eighteen years she had been walking, but with most of her potential drained—until Jesus liberated her, and she stood up straight. Note: Jesus gave her permission to stand up; she praised God, and the synagogue leader was unhappy!

The Luke passage refers to women as the oldest second-class people, but it implies many more deprived and unequal peoples. We live in a country that promises what it has not yet delivered to every individual: not to be made absolutely equal, but to have the opportunity to rise to the highest level of our quality. We need to remind ourselves occasionally in the church that the various liberation movements were not begun in our documents nor even in the movements of Martin Luther King, Jr., Betty Friedan, or third world liberationists. Liberation began in the theology of Jesus and was reborn again in the 1960s and 1970s in some of the more orthodox churches (not the evangelical ones).

The church has often been slow in assisting people to stand up straight. We are not surprised that some minority members make it into professional schools, onto corporation boards, and to the Supreme Court. But what about a black woman with little formal theological training who gets elected as an Episcopal bishop?

Many of you have shared the social and spiritual revolution of recent decades. We have shared the information bases that should raise our consciousness about the needs of the world and our people. We feel liberated by our knowledge; we really do believe that all people are gifted with aptitudes for changing our world and the church.

In effect, we have all been asked the same three questions: Where are you? Where is your brother? What is that in your hand? If the real call to do something about this world requires servanthood rather than just liberation and equality, is that an ugly word? Many college young people like the concepts of management, aggression, competition, and yuppie better. If the truth has really made you free, and the Word is within you, what in this world do you intend to do about it?

Endnotes

[1]John Naisbitt, *Megatrends* (New York: Warner Books, 1982).
[2]Harvey Cox, *Just as I Am* (Nashville: Abingdon Press, 1983).

III.
Meeting

"They have heard that you, O Lord, are in the midst of this people; for you, O Lord, are seen face to face."
(Num 14:14)

"And now I commend you to God and to the message of his grace, a message that is able to build you up and to give you the inheritance among all who are sanctified."

(Acts 20:32)

"Every one who sought the Lord would go out to the tent of meeting."
(Exodus 33:7)

"Hear, O Israel: The Lord our God is one Lord" (Deut. 6:4). With these words from the Shema, the president of Temple B'nai Israel, Jay Marx, greeted the congregation of Christian worshipers that had come to meet in its Jewish worship center. Earlier, during the Sunday School hour, Rabbi Kenneth White opened the tabernacle for the children of Northminster and explained to them the meaning of the Torah scrolls.

After two months of meetings, the people who would become Northminster Church had outgrown their second place of worship. Numerous inquiries regarding a new gathering site met with difficulties of different sorts. The congregation was rapidly running out of alternatives. Then, help came from an unexpected source.

The elected leader of the congregation of Temple B'nai Israel, Mel Cohen, learned that this small group of (mostly) Baptists needed a place in which to worship and pursue their God-given vision of starting a new church. He promptly recommended to his congregation that they invite this body of Christian believers to meet in their synagogue. Temple B'Nai Israel's acceptance of the recommendation began a very special relationship between members of these two religious fellowships, a relationship that continues into the present.

Walking into the temple to attend her new congregation's first worship service there, Dibble Pate thought, "I have returned to the roots of where all this began." Such a sensation was neither singular nor insignificant. As Ralph Webb recalls, "It was important for those of us who felt we had lost our Baptist roots to discover even more ancient roots to which we could cling."

After listening to the Northminster choir sing "Sanctus" as the Choral Introit for this special Sunday morning service, members of the congregation eagerly joined their voices in a litany that affirmed:

> If Yahweh does not fill the house, in vain the masons toil. . . . You, O God, in Christ established the church and in Christ's name we gather. And by Your Spirit You watch over Your people, giving us cause to rejoice.

Northminster Church met in the worship center of Temple B'Nai Israel from February 1989 to August 1991. On a memorable Sunday morning in this place, Cathe Webb captured the congregation's strong sentiments of both joy and sorrow in an impassioned solo presentation of the musical work "Out of My Bondage." In this temple, surrounded by reminders of God's care for the children of Israel during their long journey to a home land, the members of Northminster Church experienced God's leadership in their lives and grew in the faith that would take them home.

Every worship service in the Temple was intentionally (in contrast to conveniently) Christian. Each Saturday, members of the Northminster congregation placed a communion table at the front of the building and set on this table two candlesticks, a large gold cross, and the elements prepared for the Lord's Supper. Seasonal banners of the Christian year, designed by Keith Joiner and sewed by Keith and his wife Penny, were hung on each side of the marble unit that housed scrolls of the Torah. Then, at the conclusion of the Sunday morning worship hour each week, Northminster people removed all of the Christian symbols from the sanctuary and stored them in a curtained area on the side of the platform off Masur Hall. The weekly routine of bringing distinctively Christian symbols into a worship center designed for Jewish services heightened people's awareness of the significance of certain dimensions of Christian worship and offered a powerful, silent commentary on the differences and similarities between the two faiths.

A remarkably strong bond of friendship developed between members of these two congregations. Extended conversations with each other revealed mutual feelings of hurt. As people in the Jewish community recalled how their faith had led them into experiences of ostracism within society and even abuse as prisoners of war, Northminster people felt free to talk about the pain and sense of bondage that had so often accompanied their spiritual pilgrimage.

Sharing together on a personal level resulted in worshiping together on a corporate level, especially during Jewish festival periods like Hanukkah and Yom Kippur. Members of Temple B'Nai Israel were especially gratified and deeply moved when, in one of these shared services, the Northminster choir sang nine or ten pieces of Jewish service music, some of which were in Hebrew.

Shortly after Northminster Church began worshiping in the temple, a new rabbi came to serve there. The Northminster congregation insisted on sponsoring and hosting a large reception to introduce Rabbi David Kline, his wife Barbara Kline, and their family to the city of Monroe.

Many members of the temple fellowship continue to speak appreciatively about the positive impact that the Northminster congregation made on their corporate life during the extended period in which it met there. Northminster families needed a nursery, and the temple did not have one. So, the Northminster congregation completely outfitted a nursery and encouraged the temple congregation to use it as well. Subsequently, this new facility attracted to the temple young families who had not been involved previously. Frank Swayze remembers frying fish for a dinner jointly sponsored by the two fellowships. Members of the temple who had not been involved in its corporate life for two or three years renewed their contact by attending this event. To the amazement of both congregations, as the numbers of people attending Northminster's Sunday School classes grew, so did the numbers of people participating in the temple's educational programs.

The congregation of Temple B'Nai Israel also had a significant impact on Northminster people. On two or three occasions, the rabbi preached in a Sunday morning worship service. He was almost always present for the choir's Wednesday evening rehearsals, listening to and affirming its work. Repeatedly, lay members of B'Nai Israel attended Northminster-sponsored events and encouraged Northminster people to vigorously pursue their dream of building a worship center of their own.

Perhaps, though, the greatest benefits derived from Northminster Church meeting in the temple were intangible in nature. Learning more about Judaism caused people to re-evaluate their theological convictions, to set aside any narrow-mindedness among them, and to expand their understanding of ecumenical relations.

In its earliest days in the temple, unfettered by concerns about property and the burden of constructing a building, the Northminster congregation wisely devoted itself to lectures, dialogues, and various kinds of studies on the meaning of "being church." Members were eager to clarify the nature of their ecclesiastical identity and shape a responsible vision of ministry.

Over a period of several months, Northminster Church brought to its fellowship several resource people to lead the congregation in a wide range of biblical-theological studies related to the nature and mission of the church. Sam Sanford was first. Then came Fisher Humphreys, Will Campbell, Findley Edge, Frank Stagg, and Linda Weaver Williams to lead indepth, weekend studies.

Additionally, Northminster secured as Sunday worship leaders individuals whose ideas about church they could discover informally before and after listening to the ministers' formal presentations in their midst: Jerry Edmondson, Sarah Frances Anders, Doug Ezell, Susan Lockwood, Charles Harvey, Jr., Foy Valentine, C. B. Hastings, Katherine Allen, Betty McGehee, William Hodge, Marjorie McCullough, Walter Shurden, Betty McGary, Amy Green, Clifton Tennison, Ralph Henson, Earl Guinn, Jeanette Holt, Lacy Thompson, Liz Harris-Lamkin, Paul Stephenson, Stan Hastey, and others.

Northminster Church also looked to members of its fellowship for worship leadership through sermonic presentations: James Burns, Larry Parks, Jack Crews, Charlie Underwood, Fred Jones, and Harold Hughens filled the pulpit on different occasions. Three ministers preached in Northminster's worship services more than any others and thus influenced the congregation significantly: James Carter, an executive of the Louisiana Baptist Convention; Doug McGuire, a retired Methodist pastor; and James Lamkin, a hospital chaplain.

Meeting in the synagogue of Temple B'Nai Israel provided Northminster Church a matchless time of learning, bonding, and worshiping. Members of the Jewish congregation took great pride in aiding as well as encouraging the development of Northminster Church. As Dick Fuchs recalls, "The Jewish congregation was nicer to us than any Baptists were." The generosity and openness of the Jewish fellowship engendered these same qualities in Northminster Church.

6.
Overcoming Obstacles to Inclusions

Stan Hastey

(Because of its early association with and support for the Southern Baptist Alliance, Northminster Church maintained close contact with the leader of that organization. On Sunday, 13 September 1992, Stan Hastey led in worship and delivered the sermon in Northminster's service. Dr. Hastey continues to serve as the executive director of the Alliance of Baptists, working out of his office in Washington, D.C.)

Lest we harbor the illusion that the early church was free from the troubles so often afflicting its present-day successor institution, the Acts of the Apostles presents us with a needed corrective. Consider for a moment what these early disciples of Jesus faced:

- repeated acts of violent persecution on the part of religious traditionalists, beginning with the stoning to death of Stephen—the church's first martyr (Acts 6–7)—at the forefront of which was one Saul, a particularly devout and zealous Pharisee

- official persecution by the Roman Empire at the hand of King Herod, who had James, the brother of John, killed and arrested Peter himself (Acts 12)

- confusion, if not chaos, within the ranks of the early disciples themselves over the profound theological question of whether the grace of God in Jesus Christ was made available to non-Jews (Acts 10–11; 13–14).

Of these early crises, the third one was far and away the most difficult. Violent, bloody persecution, perpetrated by the forces of religion or the state, only succeeded in tempering the resolve of the early Christians to press forward with their divine commission. The fierceness of the debate over inclusiveness was what really threatened to undo them, however.

The inverse, and far happier, side of this history is that when they were at their best, the early Christians were distinguished in their communities by a kind of unconditional love for one another that defied the hard age in which they lived and rendered their witness—the love of God they were imitating. It ever has remained so. As youth we sang this truth and sing it still:

> We are one in the Spirit,
> We are one in the Lord. . . .
> And they'll know we are Christians
> By our love, by our love.[1]

You will remember that the early conflict over whether to include Gentiles in the orb of God's redeeming acts in Jesus Christ came to pit against one another the church's two primary leaders, Peter and Paul. Acts, chapter 10, relates the beginning of the resolution to this conflict in Peter's vision in Joppa on the roof of the house belonging to Simon the tanner. In that vision, Peter saw the heavens open, and something appearing to be a large sheet was lowered to the ground by its four corners. On the sheet were all kinds of animals, reptiles, and birds, and Peter was commanded to kill and eat from among them.

Peter refused, replying, "By no means, Lord; for I have never eaten anything that is profane or unclean" (v. 14). The unseen voice said, "What God has made clean, you must not call profane" (v. 15b). This discourse, the text tells us, occurred three times.

As he pondered the meaning of the vision, Peter was visited by a group of men sent from the city of Caesarea by a Roman centurion named Cornelius, who had had a vision of his own directing him to Peter. Cornelius, they told him, was a God-fearer held in great respect "by the whole Jewish nation" (v. 22). Peter was sufficiently intrigued by this strange confluence of events that he invited his visitors to lodge with him for the night.

On the next morning, Peter accompanied Cornelius' representatives back to Caesarea, where Cornelius welcomed him and told him of his vision and the instruction to seek Peter out. Cornelius then asked Peter to speak. If nothing else, Peter was always ready to speak. Here is what he said:

I truly understand that God shows no partiality, but in every nation anyone who fears him and does what is right is acceptable to him. (vv. 34-35)

Then, after giving his summation of the Gospel, he said,

All the prophets testify about him that everyone who believes in him receives forgiveness of sins through his name. (v. 43)

Everyone! This is the key word in Peter's homily. Then, the most amazing thing happened: "The Holy Spirit fell upon all who heard the word" (v. 44). The key word here, of course, is all. Then Peter and the other Jewish Christians baptized the new Gentile believers.

Yet the debate in the early church over inclusion of Gentiles was hardly resolved with Peter's own change of heart. Indeed, battle lines were drawn between those whose view of the grace of God was broad enough to include them as they were and those who insisted that Gentiles first become like Jews through the rite of circumcision. An unspoken dimension of this debate had to do with the place of women, who still were seen by most, if not all, of the early male disciples as second-class citizens in the church at best—but more on this later.

So determined was the exclusivist party in this battle that some people were saying, "Unless you are circumcised according to the custom of Moses, you cannot be saved" (Acts 15:1). But Paul and Barnabas, the earliest missionaries to the Gentiles, in whose presence this was said, refused to accept what they heard. Verse 2 states the situation clearly:

And after Paul and Barnabas had no small dissension and debate with them, (they) and some of the others were appointed to go up to Jerusalem to discuss this question with the apostles and the elders.

Thus the first major internal crisis in the early church came to a head in what has come to be called the Jerusalem Council. There in Jerusalem the whole matter was aired in what can only be described as a decisive moment in the history of the church. This is high drama indeed.

Why was this moment so decisive? It set the church on the irreversible course of including all of God's people regardless of race or religious background. For us, this moment was decisive for the simple reason that you and I were included too.

Not always in Christian history has the outcome of debates over inclusion been so happy. A century and a half ago, our Southern Baptist ancestors made the fateful choice of excluding their slaves from full citizenship in both temporal and spiritual realms. Their defense of the institution of human servitude became so obsessive they were willing even to separate themselves from their fellow Baptists in the North and form a new convention, a convention conceived in slavery and devoted to the perpetuation of racial division.

During the more recent turmoil that has engulfed Southern Baptists, some of us have decided the time is right to address this old issue directly. Two years ago, during the annual convocation of the Alliance of Baptists, we were unexpectedly confronted with the chance to address it when one of our founding directors brought a "statement of confession and repentance," which we proceeded to adopt unanimously. I am utterly convinced this simple action was inspired by the Spirit of God. It has had an enormously liberating effect upon us. Already, it has been read before more than one public gathering of Baptists of African-American descent, each time eliciting an absolutely electrifying response on the part of our black sisters and brothers.

In early May of this year, a group of Alliance people who were participants in the second General Assembly of the Cooperative Baptist Fellowship decided to bring the sense of this statement to that larger body of progressive Southern Baptists. We convened in Fort Worth, Texas, on Thursday, 29 April, the day following announcements of the "not guilty" verdicts in the cases of the four Los Angeles police officers accused of beating the motorist Rodney King. The first reports of the terrible violence that was to engulf the city of Los Angeles were just being filed. We framed our statement in that context, convinced it would be unconscionable for a group of Christians to be meeting during those terrible days and say nothing about the crisis in the nation.

So a director of the Alliance brought a statement of confession and repentance to the floor for consideration. Through the adoption of this statement, the Cooperative Baptist Fellowship, like the Alliance, proceeded to "publicly confess and repent of our historic complicity in condoning and perpetuating the sin of slavery before and during the Civil War" and to "hereby apologize to all African Americans for that sin." The statement went on to declare:

We reject forthrightly the racism which has persisted throughout our history as Southern Baptists, even to this present day. . . . We acknowledge with regret that . . . we are too white, too middle-class, and too insulated from the seething racial problems confronting our society. . . . (We) pledge to seek ways and means of working with our Christian sisters and brothers in the African-American churches in addressing the critical needs of all people of color.

A second issue some of us have been addressing with great intentionality in these times of transition among Baptists is that of the role of women in the church. Earlier I made note of the language in Acts 15 that makes us painfully aware that on the whole women were but an afterthought in the discussion over inclusion in the early church—if that. Indeed, the question that finally brought this fierce debate over inclusion of Gentiles to a head was that of whether Gentile believers had to be circumcised—in this context hardly a female issue!

Time will not permit a thoroughgoing examination of the status of women in Palestine in the first century A.D. or of the overall treatment of women in the larger context of the ancient world or of the Roman Empire. It must suffice to note that women generally were the objects of scorn, neglect, and abuse throughout much of society. Women had no legal status. They could not own property. Instead, they were seen as property, the possessions of men. Routinely, women were abandoned, even murdered.

Against such a bleak background, Jesus' treatment of women can only be described as revolutionary. He accorded women a status unheard of, either within Judaism or in the larger pagan society. Little wonder that women, in turn, were attracted to Jesus' teachings and became his most devoted disciples. We must not forget, after all, that women were the first evangels of resurrection good news.

In our time and context, particularly at the present moment in Baptist life, some of us have been unwilling to accept the ecclesiastical status quo concerning the role of women in the ministry of the church, whether of laywomen or women clergy. Within the Alliance, in the second of our seven guiding principles—principles we consider so important to us we call them our covenant—we have stated our commitment

to the freedom of the local church under the authority of Jesus Christ
to shape its own life and mission, call its own leadership, and ordain
whom it perceives as gifted for ministry, male or female.

I cannot fail to address one other issue of inclusion within the church
in our time. Some persons are calling this looming crisis in the churches
the most difficult one since slavery. I refer to homosexuality.

Many, if not all, of you are aware that during this year, two churches
affiliated with both the Southern Baptist Convention and the Alliance of
Baptists took actions involving gays who are members of those congregations, one voting to bless the union of gay men and lesbians, the other to
license to the gospel ministry a gay divinity student.

I want you to know in all candor that I do not know how I would
have voted in either case had I been a member of those churches. I do
know, though, that for me these are no longer easy issues, although once
they would have been. At one time, I would have been staunchly opposed
to the actions taken by both of these churches.

What has caused me in more recent years to ponder the questions of
whether and to what extent openly homosexual persons should be included in the life of the church is intensely personal. I began to be faced with
such questions directly one night several years ago when one of my
younger siblings, a brother, called out of the blue to inform me he is gay.
He asked that I tell the rest of the family. I did, and all of us have been
dealing with questions concerning homosexuality in an entirely different
light ever since.

When he called, my brother said he had known of his sexual orien-
tation since about age ten. This brother of mine, this son of missionary
parents, is a professing Christian. He is a caring, generous, and sensitive
person. I can no longer laugh at the cruel jokes about homosexuals. No
longer can I assume that all homosexual persons deliberately choose to
be gay or lesbian. I have come to a point of determination about oppos-
ing and speaking out against all forms of gay-bashing.

All of this is not to say I have all the answers, for I do not. I remain
perplexed about many issues surrounding homosexuality. Nor do I pre-
sume to know precisely how the church should respond in every instance.
But I am willing to listen and learn in the hope that the day will come
when answers are clearer. If the day comes, as I believe it will, when the
evidence is incontrovertible that homosexuality is more a genetic given

than a chosen lifestyle, I hope we in the church will do better about reconciling scripture with modernity than we have done in the debates over slavery and women.

For now, I am driven back to the lesson that was learned the hard way by the early church about the despised Gentiles, a lesson that happens to square nicely with the words of an old gospel song, words that express a truth for which I am profoundly grateful:

> Jesus included me,
> Yes, he included me,
> When the Lord said "Whosoever,"
> He included me.[2]

I would add only this thought: If Jesus included me, who am I to build up obstacles to the inclusion of anyone else? Amen.

Endnotes

[1]Peter Scholtes, "They'll Know We Are Christians by Our Love," *The Hymnal for Worship and Celebration*, ed. Tom Fettke (Waco: Word Music, 1986) 284.

[2]Johnson Oatman, Jr. "He Included Me," *The Baptist Hymnal*, ed. Wesley L. Forbis (Nashville: Convention Press, 1991) 436.

7.
Let God Be God

Exodus 3:13-22

Michelle Toole

(In the summer of 1990, Michelle Toole filled the pulpit of Northminster Church several times. Dr. Toole is an instructor at The Southern Baptist Theological Seminary and Bellarmine College in Louisville, Kentucky.)

When I was in the fourth grade, my friends and I discovered the power of story, especially in the form of drama. I do not remember learning any special facts in school that year, but I do remember writing plays and acting in plays. In fact, it seems like that is all we ever did—at least that is what I remember. Being the great Bible scholars that we were, many of our plays centered around Bible characters—the familiar stories that we studied year in and year out in Sunday School.

In the fourth grade, I had my first starring role in a Christmas play. Usually I was a sheep or a tree or the innkeeper's wife, but never, never Mary. Mary was always my good friend, Jill Barnett. She was blond, blue-eyed, quiet, and certainly not as mischievous as I was. I was not Mary material. But this year, for some reason, I was Mary. I knew my lines and practiced holding the baby doll Jesus. I convinced myself that I could do it. I could be Mary.

The day came. Parents, visitors, and classmates crowded into a classroom. The play went well. No angels lost their halos, no wise men's robes fell off. Everyone said their lines. The lights dimmed, and the spotlight was turned on Joseph, baby Jesus, and me. Now, my big moment.

I had to sing "Away in a Manger." I was paralyzed with fear. Suddenly, I knew why Jill had always been Mary. She could sing solos, and I could not. I wanted the earth to open up and swallow me. Somehow I croaked out the song, shaking so badly that I nearly dropped baby Jesus. I survived, but just barely. Never again did I choose to play Mary.

In spite of my traumatic experience, I still recognized the power and magic of the story. The story came alive for us in that fourth grade classroom. Even with the time-worn familiarity of the Christmas story, it was still magic. It revealed what God was like.

Just within the framework of the Christmas story, we see the kind of God who shared the message about the in-breaking of the kingdom of God with three travel-worn wise men and a group of smelly shepherds, a God who chose a young peasant girl to be the mother of the Messiah, a God who demonstrated what it means to be a free and loving human being by sending a son to dwell among us, a God who communicates love through the weak and powerless. Yes, the Christmas story is a very big story.

The other big story in the Bible is the story of Moses and the exodus —another dramatic story that tells what God is like—a story of deliverance from suffering and oppression, redemption, and liberation in this world. This story, too, was one of our fourth grade favorites with several great dramatic moments: Moses floating in a basket and being rescued by a princess, Moses arguing with God, the plagues, the crossing of the Red Sea, forty years of wandering, the golden calf, crossing into the promised land. Yes, Exodus is a big story for Christians and Jews. It tells us what God is like.

A few months ago I saw a plaque in a bookstore that read, "Let God be God." I wondered then, as I still do, what it means. "Let God be God." It is definitely an admirable sentiment, and no one could disagree. What could be more important than letting the true God be God for you? Letting God be God presupposes that we know some of who and what God is, when we allow God to be God in our lives. But, how in the world do you discover who God is, so that you can let God be God?

We begin to know who God is by looking at stories—the story of your life, how God has been active in your life and experiences, or the life story of other people such as saints, heroes, family, and friends.

On Wednesday night, Jim Files was telling us about his grandmother, who ran a boarding house. She was warm-hearted and hospitable. Jim learned about faith and God from knowing his grandmother and being a part of her life.

We respond to stories. Through stories we see who God is, who Jesus is. The Old Testament lesson of the story of Moses gives us clues as to who God is. First, God is mystery.

We try to make God our possession. God is American, Protestant, Southern, Baptist. We try to remake God in our own image, to put God in a neat little box that fits comfortably with our lifestyles and values. If God is just like us, why do we need to grow or change? If God is just like us, then letting God be God is very easy. But God is greater than our descriptions, different than our pictures painted by self-interest, more than our words.

God is like a diamond with many facets. We can identify characteristics and qualities, but God remains beyond description, surprising, a mystery. Throughout the Bible, we see different images and names for God: Father, Creator, Lord, Friend, Mother, Shepherd. God is all of these and more. God cannot be pinned down to one image, one role, or one name. God does not seem to care too much what people call God, as long as lines of communication are always kept open.

In response to Moses' question "Who are you?" God gave an answer that was both a personal name and a puzzle. No one is quite sure what it means: "I am who I am" (Exod 3:14) ("I will be who I will be"). God's answer speaks of present force and continuing presence. It speaks of God's hiddeness and mystery.

When we speak of God, all we do is frame the silence. We accept the mystery with gratitude and wonder. We see clues of who God is through God's interaction with people. We do not understand all about life or all about God. We have questions about suffering, the universe, and the human body. We do not stop asking questions, but we do accept that there will always be questions and mystery.

God is also accessible. God's answer to Moses was mysterious, but it revealed God's personal name, Yahweh. Giving a name in the Old Testament culture gave power and control. One's name revealed character and disclosed identity.

God continued by connecting God's identity to the past. This is the same God Abraham, Isaac, and Jacob worshiped—three very different persons. Abraham took his wife and servants to a new and strange land as he followed Jehovah. Jacob was both pious and dishonest, devout and treacherous. Isaac was quiet, contemplative, and ordinary. God is the God of all three types of persons, with no favorites.

God related to these three men in three different ways. The angel of God wrestled with Jacob when he asked for a blessing. God led Abraham to a strange and wonderful land and promised that he would be a parent of a great nation. To Isaac, God was a fear—unanticipated possibilities.

Moses discovered that God was accessible. When God first spoke to Moses, Moses was a shepherd with his father-in-law's sheep—certainly a step down from the Pharaoh's palace—but Moses felt the freedom to argue with God. Throughout the stories in the Exodus, Moses questioned, disagreed, argued, and begged God. Moses instinctively knew that Yahweh was accessible.

This accessibility freed Moses to be an imperfect person and frees us to be the imperfect people that we are. We do not have to be supermen or superwomen. We can be weak. We can lay our burdens before God. We can tell our fears and know that God will respond to us. After all, when Moses told God, "Not me, I can't talk in front of crowds," God provided Aaron's help. God will give us Aarons, as well, because God knows that we are fearful folks.

God is the *deliverer*. God not only said, "I will be with you," but God promised deliverance. God cared about the blight of the Israelites who were oppressed in Egypt. In the first three chapters of the book of Exodus, slavery is described as an affliction, a burden, and a sorrow. Slavery was active and personal. Pharaoh was never called a tyrant, but in Jewish literature he was known as the first of all tyrants—a Hitler of ancient Egypt.

Clearly the Israelites were in bondage, described as work without end that both degraded and exhausted the slaves. They were in bondage from without and within. They had, undoubtedly, developed a slave mentality. They were afraid of their masters, subservient and crushed by oppression.

The Israelites struggled to survive. Their baby sons had been killed. They had been forced to be slaves in a country where they had been citizens. They must have wondered where God was. God said,

> I have also seen how the Egyptians oppress them. . . . I will send you
> to Pharaoh to bring my people . . . out of Egypt. (Exod 3:9-10)

God used one who did not suffer from a slave mentality. Martin Buber said that the exodus was not the kind of revolution that could be led by a slave. Moses had grown up in the palace of the Pharoah.

The good news for the Israelites and the good news for us is that the world is not all Egypt. God will deliver us from Egypt. We all have Egypts that oppress us: financial burdens, relational problems, emotional afflictions, and political crises. We call them by names and think that because we are not physically present in a jail we are not enslaved, but the results are the same.

After struggling with our burdens, we see ourselves as worthless, powerless, and in bondage. We are tired and apathetic as a result of discouraging circumstances and past failures. Like the Israelites, we can internalize the truth that the world is not all Egypt. God can and will deliver us. God will cleanse the doors of our perception, so that we can see and experience deliverance and freedom.

It is interesting that the Israelites' experience in slavery, their oppression at the hand of the Egyptians, was reflected in their laws and religious rituals. They did not repress the memory of injustice. They remembered it. The Israelites were commanded to act justly, not as their Egyptian taskmasters acted. Their negative experience in slavery helped shape a positive moral code. Their relationship with God dramatically affected the treatment of strangers, neighbors, widows, orphans, parents, servants, and the poor.

God delivered the Israelites out of Egypt, and the people responded by acting justly, by affirming their intention to keep God's commandment. In the same way, our past can influence our present and future. We learn from all kinds of experiences: successes, failures, joys, and pains. Remembering the past can help us to be more compassionate, forgiving, and loving. We do not repress the past and bury our secrets. We help others to benefit from our experience.

From Exodus we also learn that God leads and directs us on our journeys. God told Moses that not only would the Israelites be delivered from Egypt, but they would be led to the promised land—the land flowing with milk and honey—and the only way to get to the promised land was through the wilderness.

God does not intend that we be puppet people. We have the freedom to choose and to act. We are not the mindless pawns of a powerful God. God gifts us with freedom—freedom to choose our directions, freedom to be partners with God in bringing in the kingdom of God, freedom to struggle and to walk on different paths.

We see from the story of the Israelites that they did not always make wise choices. They yearned for the familiarity of Egypt. They worshiped a golden calf. They were not magically transported to the promised land. The people marched to get there, and the march was full of difficulties, crises, and struggles. Their journeys and our journeys seem very slow, with two steps forward and one step back.

We follow a God who does lead and direct us, but not as a dictator prescribing one path. Sometimes we do not know that God has led us until after the fact. Often we only see God's activity with clarity after we have come through the crises, the plagues, the crossing of the Red Sea, the wandering in the wilderness, or whatever our equivalent may be.

In his book *Exodus and Revolution,* Michael Walzer said that there is no way to get to the promised land except by joining together and marching, by acting as a community, by fulfilling our mission, and beginning our journey. We follow where God leads as individuals, but we also follow God and discover who God is in a community of faith. We need each other's insights to give us light for the journey. We need each other's support and encouragement to help us live. We are all needy persons. We need each other, and we need God.

Let God be God—a good goal, a challenge to identify who our God is. Is God the one we have made or the one who made us? God challenges us to renounce the little gods we have made and serve Yahweh, the true God. We unmask the gods who do not have the power to sustain and fulfill our lives. We have no other gods before Jehovah God.

As we reflect on our life stories and the stories in the Bible, we are challenged to love, serve, and worship the God of the faithful—the God of Abraham, Isaac, Sarah, Miriam, Paul, Aquila, and Priscilla; the God of each of you; the God who is mystery, but is here for us to touch; the God who delivers us from oppressive conditions and leads and directs us as we press forward on the journey of life.

IV.
Possessing

"You shall take possession of the land and settle in it, for I have given you the land to possess it."
(Num 33:53)

"But will God dwell indeed reside with mortals on the earth? Even, heaven and the highest heaven cannot contain you, how much less this house that I have built!"

(2 Chron 6:18)

"God did not give us a spirit of cowardice, but rather a spirit of power and of love and of self-discipline."
(2 Tim 1:7)

Every significant advance in the development of Northminster Church occurred much earlier than even the most forward-looking people anticipated and unfolded at a speed that inspired amazement. Praise to God!

Nudges, pushes, and outright shoves prompted major steps in the progression of the congregation. Rational explanations for these motivations took into account the importance of personal and institutional concerns, but reason alone could not spin an understandable story. Mystery was necessary—that element of explanation that causes a hearer to experience a hush before whispering, "Oh, I see." D. H. Clark articulated the recognition, "If I ever doubted the hand of God being involved in something, it would have gone out the window here." God was behind, in, and in front of the nudges, pushes, and shoves that prodded Northminster Church forward.

Possessing the Land

In the spring of 1989, several church members began conversations about the congregation building a childcare center. Mixed motives sustained an exploration of this idea. The church wanted to employ Don Nixon who, with his wife Cathe, was on a sabbatical until the end of May. Cathe was trained and skilled in childcare. If the church established this center, Cathe could direct its ministries, and Don could serve the church. Besides, it would propel the church into a very beneficial ministry.

Members of the church asked Ralph Pritcher to chair a committee charged with finding a suitable plot of land on which the church could build a childcare center. The land had to be affordable, a caveat that made the task an incredibly tough one.

As the search for a building site proceeded, the church rethought the development the center, deciding that such a ministry initiative was not a good idea at the time. Kay Southern found an ideal location on which the church could construct a worship center, offices, and educational facilities in the future. The problem was that the building site was so absolutely ideal that paying the purchase price for the land seemed entirely out of the question for a young congregation of less than 100 members. Nevertheless, Kay contacted the owner of the land, Ben Peters, and expressed the church's interest in it. To her complete surprise, Ben Peters responded with the remark, "Let's work it out."

Legal and financial arrangements had to be made between Ben Peters and representatives of Northminster Church. As for the matter of working out the purchase, though, Kay understood the process best: "God was working in it."

Northminster Church purchased this prime piece of property for $236,000, having raised $50,000 for a down payment. Along with the decision to acquire the property came the church's informal, though firm, resolve not even to attempt to build on it for at least five years.

Not everybody in the congregation supported Ron Stewart's successfully-passed motion to negotiate the purchase of land. One man said, "We felt like the children of Israel leaving Egypt and going to the promised land." Another man vigorously opposed the purchase, however, arguing that it was much too early in the church's life to buy land. When the church voted to buy the land, this opponent of the action dropped out of the fellowship and, though encouraged to return, never did actively participate in the life of the church again. Most people in the church wanted to proceed with the purchase of the land, though they felt what the church's treasurer expressed in retrospect: "It scared me to death."

At the conclusion of the Palm Sunday worship service in 1990, having reaffirmed their church covenant and listened to Frank Stagg speak about the church's ministry of reconciliation, members of Northminster left the meeting place of Temple B'Nai Israel and boarded a bus that took them to the advent location of Northminster Church. On the plot of ground just across from Bayou Desiard at the corner of Lamy Lane and Loop Road, a small white tent covered the bread and wine of communion. A large urn set on each side of the tent. Processing behind the cross, which had been taken from the temple, Northminster members gathered in front of the communion table. They offered this litany of dedication:

> Desiring to offer to a growing community a house of prayer, we dedicate our dreams and desires as called partners in Christ's service for the possibilities of this land. . . . We dedicate this earth to the source of all truths. . . . We dedicate this place for the breaking down of walls and the acceptance of all God's people.

Then, for the first time on this new land, as they did their first time together anywhere, all the people present shared in the sacred act of Christian communion.

Building on the Land

A little over six months after Northminster Church dedicated its newly purchased land, the congregation, which had resolved not even to consider any building plans for this site for a period of at least five years, gathered again on this beautiful piece of earth to break ground for the construction of a new building. Once more the congregation devoted its best efforts to a project that seemed "untimely born."

The people of Northminster Church had settled into the facilities of Temple B'Nai Israel for a lengthy stay. Once again, however, events were moving with greater rapidity than anyone expected, with a speed that some people actually could not tolerate. Some Northminster members expressed an interest in securing a pastor prior to proceeding with a building, but that was a minority point of view. Most people in the church liked the idea of continuing to act as a pastor to each other.

Most every Northminster member dreaded more indebtedness. At the same time, however, they were eager to get on with building plans. A few individuals, like Dick Fuchs, expressed a concern that the church would not grow until the congregation was on its own.

When the committee appointed to find a piece of rental property for the church's use (chaired by Frank Swayze) reported that no suitable buildings were available, deliberations about a meeting place intensified. Finally, while figuring and doodling on a napkin during a church meeting, Walker Glenn, whose livelihood was tied to building construction, said, "We can build a modest building for $150,000. I can do it for $35 a square foot." Walker's words sounded good, but the church still owed $180,000 on its purchase of land. How else, though, could Northminster Church be out of the Temple by the end of 1990? Members of the congregation asked Ralph Asbury to chair a committee commissioned to secure financing for a building.

Walker asked Hannah Clark to draw a set of plans for a long building, this being the least costly style of building to construct. Everyone stressed that the facility would have to be simple, not fancy, a basic cement block structure—but not a structure that looked like a nursing

home, Mary Lou Rountree insisted. Hannah retreated to a beach and
spent a week drawing plans for a building with 7,800 square feet. Kay
Southern also drew a set of plans, which turned out to be within 200
square feet of the plans drawn by Hannah. Walker secured bids on construction costs, using a plan that had been drawn on a piece of poster
paper.

Several people in the church speak of the present structure as Hannah Clark's building, an assertion with which Hannah argues. The highly
regarded anesthesiologist explains:

> I'm just an amateur architect who has read some books. . . I'm a nuts
> and bolts person. I'm not a spiritual leader here. This is when the nuts
> and bolts people got to shine.

Hannah praises the influence of Northminster Church:

> We find talents here. Then, we empower people to do what they have
> never done. I had always wanted to be an architect, and I finally got to
> be one.

On the first Sunday in October, 1990, Northminster Church gathered
in Temple B'Nai Israel as usual for the worship of God. This day was
different, though. After Frank Stagg spoke to the congregation about
"The Impulse to Security and Venture," the group prepared to travel to
the lot owned by the church and there to break ground for the construction of its first building.

Worshipers were reminded that on this day of celebration for them,
many people in other parts of the world were hurting. The congregation
remembered particularly Americans held hostage in the Middle East and
their families. Each worshiper wore a yellow ribbon as a symbol of "consciousness of hostage people" and "as a reminder that they wait and must
depend on our efforts in setting them free." With the choir singing, "Go-
in' Home" from Dvorak's *New World Symphony*, worshipers filed out of
the temple and struck out toward the site of their new building.

A huge urn of greenery stood at each of the four corners of the
church's property. All the people present took up positions on the land
so as to outline the planned perimeter of the new building. Children of
the congregation gathered in the center of the crowd and talked with Don

Nixon about the meaning of breaking ground. Then, together the people spoke to God:

> O God, make us ever mindful of each person's special contribution to the life of this your church. We stand in awe, O God, of the wondrous skills here assembled: the encompassing eye of the planner, the tempered patience of the crafter and engineer, the calloused hands of the builder who labors for the common good. O God, let no talent be overlooked . . . cast your Spirit among us this day. Let us be builders of a holy temple: a place where humans may find peace in the face of turmoil, yet not a place where complacency finds a home. Let us be servants and visionaries both: planters and harvesters each, stewards of a living treasure. O God, make the seeds we plant this day call forth a bounteous crop, and let the fruit of that crop be our lives dedicated to you now and ever more. Amen.

Every person had a shovel and participated in digging up the earth to prepare for a new church building. With clumps of freshly dug earth lying all around, the people sang "The Church's One Foundation" and enjoyed their first meal together at home: the bread and wine of Christian communion.

Because of a lack of the fire marshal's approval of the building plans, a building permit was not issued to the church until late in December. By that time, rains had set in to the extent that a slab could not be poured until April 1991.

Concerns related to the construction of the new building produced major stresses within the congregation. Almost everybody had an idea, or at least an opinion, about the planned building; and almost everybody in the church showed up at the construction site every day. Over the course of several turbulent months, this congregation had negotiated many difficult situations successfully. The erection of a new building constituted a challenge to the unity of the fellowship like no other, however.

Members of the congregation made several cost-cutting decisions up front. For example, the people decided they could save daily clean-up costs at the construction site by doing the clean-up work themselves. For theological as well as economic reasons, members wanted the church building to convey openness by the use of clear windows, rather than costly stained glass.

Walker Glenn promised the church that he would bring this project to a conclusion without exceeding the budgeted amount for it, and he was not about to break that promise. Though some individuals got their feelings hurt by Walker's hard line policy, the builder watched every expenditure closely and rejected suggested alterations that would increase the price of the building.

When various individuals in the congregation started asking serious questions about adjustments in the building plans and discussing the possibility of making additions of various kinds, Walker developed another policy that he enforced with stern inflexibility: "If you want it different, you have to pay for it"—and a check for the expenditure had to be written on the spot. Many people gave a lot of money for enhancements to the building, and no one requested a plaque of recognition—a request that would have been turned down had it been made.

Susan Curry, Hannah Clark, and others saw to it that the building looked good. Time and time again, Susan advocated a certain aesthetic touch and found someone to fund it, often herself. At one point, Susan lobbied for a design process to make the concrete floors in the worship center look like marble. She volunteered the services of her husband, Jimmy Curry, who she was sure could do this work, though he had never done anything like it before—and he did it, with help from Peggy Burns. Jimmy and Peggy devoted innumerable hours and incredible energy to a project that brought unimagined beauty to the sanctuary.

Though virtually every member of Northminster Church made a substantial contribution to the construction of the new church building, no person's involvement was more significant than that of Walker Glenn. Northminster could not have afforded the building that stands today had it not been constructed by him. He stopped everything else he was doing and spent three months without pay working on Northminster's building. Additionally, he called in every favor he had ever earned in the building trade. Subsequently, many building materials were sold to the church at a greatly reduced price.

The period of construction work on the new building coincided with a time of extreme hardship in the community of Monroe. Massive flooding displaced people throughout the city. Several Northminster families had to move into temporary housing arrangements because their homes were under water. During these days, work on the church building took second place to doing the work of the church in relation to people in need.

A major enhancement to the beauty of the sanctuary and its functional importance as a worship center resulted from the generosity of D. H. Clark. Ten years earlier, he had purchased a very unique pipe organ for his house—a tracker organ made by the Moller Company, one of that firm's few trackers. D. H. had this organ moved from his house and installed in the sanctuary of Northminster Church's new facility.

The room that Northminster Church constructed as a sanctuary for worship reflects the priority that the congregation assigns to public worship as well as its priorities in corporate worship. An elevated antique pulpit is on one side of a divided chancel, and a gold lectern on the other. At the center of the chancel stands a communion table from which members of the congregation take the bread and the cup weekly— elements at the center of the congregation's pilgrimage since its first informal gathering—and offer them to all who come forward to eat and drink Christ's provisions. Gold candlesticks and a large cross, which one of the members brought from another congregation, also attract worshipers' attention to the communion table.

The absence of a baptistry in the sanctuary is an exception to the room's reflection of the church's theology. Baptisms at Northminster are joyous occasions when members of the fellowship line the banks of a bayou to watch the immersion of new Christians in the waters of the bayou and celebrate their new life.

As the building project neared completion, the Northminster fellowship realized that it had made its way through another potentially trying time with no major scars. Norma Hickman remembers her amazement that "Everyone was in agreement: No bickering!" Enthusiasm pervaded the fellowship. People were astounded by the facility that had been constructed.

After going through the new building, a local business man estimated that the church had spent a minimum of $800,000 on this structure. In reality, Walker Glenn completed the building at a cost of $175,000. The beauty of the facility defied accurate monetary figures. Only recently, when the Northminster worship center was included in the "Winterfest Tour of Homes" in Monroe, a brochure advertizing the event called attention to the building's unhidden air conditioning ducts and concrete flooring as "aspects of the design and ultimately a unifying point of the design," concluding "Northminster's simplicity of detail and its lack of pretense give to the structure an elegance not usually seen in temporal structures."

The intensity of the joy produced by the new building was exceeded only by an eagerness to begin worship within it and to get on with being church. Some folks were concerned that the church's priorities not get out of order. An interest in the looks of the new church building could not suffice for a commitment to the substance indicative of, indeed unique to, a church.

On Sunday, 18 August, 1991, after a time of worship in Temple B'Nai Israel, members of Northminster boarded a bus that carried them to their new building. Though the building was still not completely finished, and the local fire marshall had not yet approved permanent occupancy of the structure, Northminster members were eager to express words of dedication and feelings of celebration in their new place of worship.

When the worshipers arrived at their new home place, they found Rabbi David Kline standing before them at the front door of the church building. Rabbi Kline explained that the Jewish congregation had nurtured these people in their house much as a parent would nurture a child, but that it was now time for these Christians to be on their own. The rabbi said, "I cannot go any further with you. I have walked as far as I can walk with you." After the rabbi blessed the Northminster people, the doors of the new building were opened, and the congregation moved inside to receive the bread and wine of Christian communion.

After plans for the first service in the new building were made and changed several times, finally the day of celebration arrived. On 8 September, 1991, Northminster Church dedicated its new building with numerous guests present and Frank Stagg preaching. What a festive day!

The New Testament lesson was accompanied by the words, "The God of new beginnings has called us to this place." Members of the congregation declared in one voice, "We will be shouters of joy and seekers of God's light wherever we go. Praise God for this day!" Along with several other pieces of music, the choir sang, "Arise Your Light Has Come" by Danner, "Let the People Praise Thee, O Lord" by Mathias, "I Was Glad When They Said Unto Me" by Parry, and Randall Thompson's "Alleluia."

By means of a litany, the people participated in the dedication of the building. Praise to God was expressed for the joy that is found in the church:

> for communion with one another, for the sharing of bounty and of burden; for nurturing, one generation of the next; for the expressions of holiness made visible in our midst.

Thanksgiving to God was offered:

> for the strengths which have brought this day into being: the vision, the laborers, and the dutious service of today's children of God who would cast tomorrow's church.

Prayerfully, the people requested,

> O God, make that which we begin this day to be etched upon our hearts so that nothing can separate the joy, the pride, the determination, and the love we feel at this moment for each other and for you, the cornerstone at Northminster Church. Amen.

With a celebration of Christian communion, a commission to service, and a choral presentation of Willan's "The Apostolic Benediction," Northminster Church's first worship service in its new facility concluded. The work that properly belongs to God's people at home began—no, continued.

8.
Impulse to Venture and Security

Psalm 24
Matthew 14:22-31

Frank Stagg

(Under a brilliant blue autumn sky, on 7 October 1990, Northminster Church broke ground for the construction of its first building. Frank Stagg delivered the message in the Sunday morning service.)

I had preached for over fifty years before my first attempt to preach a sermon on Peter's attempt to walk on water. I had neither the inclination nor courage for it. My problem was not with miracle as such, for we live daily in the presence of wonder. On the cosmic scale, why is there something and not nothing? Think of mutation, not just the emergence of new species but how something as commonplace as sight can arise out of energy, chemistry, or whatever. There is even the miracle of how we can somehow trigger such simple action as choosing to open or close a hand. It was not the problem of miracles in the Gospels, some miracles of compassion and some as signs pointing from one level of reality to a higher one, as when Jesus healed a man born blind and then offered sight at a higher level. But why is this story found only in Matthew? Here is the amazing story of a man nicknamed "Rock" who wanted to walk on water!

The catalyst for me was a probing conversation with a former student, Don Ritzer, as he drove me from his church in Wanesboro, Virginia, to the airport in Washington, D.C. It was a serendipity for me as he led me into a discussion of this text, with focus upon the impulses to venture and then to security.

When Peter saw Jesus walking upon the water, in his impulse to venture he cried out, "Lord, if it be you, bid me come to you walking on the water" (v. 28). Next, as he began to sink, he cried out, "Lord, save me" (v. 30). This is the impulse to security. The deeper lesson of the story, informed throughout the New Testament, is that the real venture is not in walking upon water but in commitment to go to Jesus. The real security is not in the boat, but also in Jesus.

Both impulses, to venture and to security, are not only deeply embedded in life, but both are valid. The impulse to venture requires no defense, for all of us esteem it as an idea. Following it as a practice is something else. The impulse to security is more vulnerable to blame; but it, too, has its place. The impulse to security is written deep in nature as can be seen in plant and animal life as well as in humans. See the oak tree bearing millions of acorns in its lifetime, seeking to insure its survival in its posterity. See the birds building their nests beyond the reach of predators. See the wily buck so elusive in hunting season. Evelyn and I, more interested in seeing than killing these beautiful animals, have from a deer stand at nearby Winter Quarters counted up to a hundred doe and not a buck in sight! As such, the impulse to security, at whatever level, has its proper place. There is a proper place in human life for both impulses, that to venture and that to security.

Both impulses are implied in Psalm 24:1, "To YHWH belongs the earth, the habitable world and those who dwell in it." This is security. Then follows, "For he grounded it upon the seas, and upon the subterranean streams he established it." This is venture. We would have expected, "for he grounded it upon the Rock of Gibraltar," instead of upon the ebb and flow of tides or deep underground currents.

The impulses to venture and security relate to one another in various patterns. We will examine three of them. There is the competitive pattern, where the more of one there is the less of the other. The higher the venture, the less the security. The higher the impulse to security, the lower the venture.

Sitting on the deck of our son's cabin on Fish Lake out from Talkeetna, Alaska, and looking across at Denali (commonly called Mount McKinley), I read the awesome story of Art Davidson. Many people had climbed this highest peak in America in the summer, but Art Davidson undertook it in mid winter. That is the impulse to venture, and it reduces the impulse to security to almost zero. Security people like me read the book; we do not try to climb the peak, certainly not at 148 degrees below zero.

Another example, just having happened, is the death of Stefano Casiraghi who, in the World Offshore Championship Speedboat Racing, was killed when he was traveling at ninety-three miles per hour and crashed into the side of a wave. As a boater, I well know that as venture goes up, security goes down, and vice versa.

A second pattern in the relationship of venture and security may be called ambiguous or variable. Farming is an example. To plant and cultivate a crop is a venture seeking security. It may pay off in security, but it also may be a disaster. A business investment is a venture seeking security, but it may lead to financial security or bankruptcy.

A third pattern of relationship may be termed paradoxical. In this pattern, security is offered only in venture. This is the security that Jesus offers. This is the venture/security that is the concern of this sermon.

Jesus' basic call is, "Follow me!" This call appears from the first chapter of Mark to the final chapter of John. Jesus did not stop with "Believe!" or "Confess!" These are not ultimate claims, and the latter especially is easy. A confession of faith may cost little or nothing, and it may signify little or nothing. It is a call to high adventure when Jesus says, "You follow me!" A glance at his agenda, his way, and especially his eviction from his home synagogue in Nazareth and his being nailed to a cross should be compelling evidence that the real venture is in commitment to follow Jesus. Less obvious but equally real, the only ultimate security we have is in the venture of following Jesus.

The paradox of security only in venture is explicit in Jesus' teaching: "Whoever wishes to save his or her life will destroy it, but whoever loses his or her life for my sake and the gospel's will save it!" (Mark 8:35). This followed Jesus' challenge, "If anyone wishes to follow after me, let him or her deny himself or herself and take up his or her cross and follow me" (v. 34).

The attempt to save oneself is the impulse to security, but it is doomed to failure. The self-serving principle is false and futile. In fact, it is counter-productive. Life turned inward upon itself will self-destruct. Only in losing life to God and others is life secured. Paradoxically, we receive by giving and live by dying. The grasping hand is always empty; the giving hand is full. The Cross is not just a place of death; it is in fact the way of life and to life.

The call to follow Jesus is a call to the venture of faith. It is the faith that inquires, the faith that seeks knowledge. It is not to be confused with the confession of a creed, a vain impulse to security. A creed is death to inquiry, thus death to faith.

The call to follow Jesus is a call to the venture of servanthood. The world seeks security in ruling; Jesus taught that security and greatness are in servanthood (Mark 10:35-45).

The call to follow Jesus is the call to peace and peacemaking. The impulse to security turns to swords, guns, and bombs. Jesus warned that those taking the sword perish by the sword—the very sword in one's hand. With the point of a sword, one may take another's life. With the handle in one's hand, one takes one's own life at the deeper level. Security is in the venture of peace and peacemaking, not in violence and war.

On and on it goes! Security is in the venture of new wineskins when the wine is threatened by leaky skins. Security is in the venture of rejection of the tyranny of things, not in the impulse to security in bondage to things, being owned by what we think we own. Security is in the venture of including the rejects of culture and religion, not in the impulse to security in excluding those whom Jesus included. Security is in the bold venture of trust and love, being accessible and thus vulnerable to those who can hurt us. So the paradox goes! Security is only in venture.

Erecting a building upon this land upon which we now stand is a venture of faith. What we intend to do in and through the building is the greater venture. In it let us continue the quest for our true identity and mission, values and principles, and agenda in a world where God-forsakenness is there alongside godliness, where there is alienation as well as koinonia, where power is abused but may also be used for good, where there is massive poverty and also the impulse to feed the hungry and care for the sick. Let us continue our quest in a world entrusted to our care but which is being depleted and polluted, but which can be the garden God intended it to be. We do not have to choose between venture and security, for in authentic following of Jesus there is security in venture. Let us pray, "Lord, if it be you, bid us come to you!"

9.

Churches and Church Houses

Mark 11:15-19

Frank Stagg

(Northminster Church celebrated its new house on 8 September 1991. On this day of thanksgiving, festivities, and commitment, the church requested Frank Stagg to deliver the sermon for the morning.)

Celebration of Northminster's First House

We gather this day to celebrate Northminster's first church house! It is almost a truism to say that churches and church houses are not one and the same. Although they are distinct, and we all know it, there yet is the tendency to confuse them. If a stranger inquires, "Where is Northminster Church?" anyone of us might give directions to a street address. To this point the confusion is not serious and even logistically helpful. How a given church and its church house relate is a more important and difficult matter.

Churches and houses are so distinct that either may exist without the other. A church can be without a house. So it was for Northminster Church until now. So it was for early churches for at least 200 years. The earliest Christians were Jews, and already they had a heritage of houses —a Temple in Jerusalem and synagogues wherever as many as ten heads of houses chose to gather on Sabbaths and other days.

With the destruction of the Temple in 70 C.E. and expulsion from the synagogues sometime later over the divisive issue of the inclusion of Gentiles, and with subsequent persecution under the Roman government, early Christian churches were without buildings constructed as "church houses" for two centuries or more. They worshiped and engaged in their other activities in private homes or rented buildings.

Only after Constantine added Christianity to his harem of religions did Christians have the freedom and encouragement to erect their own buildings. For more than two centuries, these churches did amazingly well without the benefit of "church houses." Even so, as "house churches," they were served by houses of some kind. There can be churches without houses, but a house can significantly serve a church. This is on the condition that as God's house, it is "a place of prayer for all nations" (Mark 11:17).

Sadly enough, there are church houses without churches. Some are buildings left empty by some church that moved or died. Some are church houses converted to other uses. Worst of all, there are gatherings called churches that meet in buildings called church houses but bear little resemblance to the Church that Jesus created; some of these are simply exclusive religious clubs.

Houses can serve a church in many ways: as a place of worship, fellowship, study, and various forms of ministry. Ideally, such a house is a medium that helps a church establish its identity and carry out its ministry. Unfortunately, sometimes a church house or complex of buildings does more to defeat the nature and purpose of the church than serve it. A building sometimes diverts or exhausts the resources of a church, limiting or defeating its proper life and ministry. Most often this situation happens in terms of the loss of a prophetic ministry lest such "rocking of the boat" result in loss of income, so important to paying off building debts and maintaining expensive property.

Paradigms from Sea Shells

The various kinds of relationships between a church and its house may be illustrated in the paradigms of sea shells and the little creatures that make or occupy sea shells. The shells and creatures that make or occupy them are not one and the same. Most of us know more about the shells than the creatures that make or occupy them.

I am not a malacologist, a specialist in the soft-bodied creatures that grow sea shells and grow in sea shells, but I do have a layperson's fascination with this area of study. Evelyn and I got our first serious interest in sea shells from Peggy Elmore, whose husband was then the pastor of the First Baptist Church in Corpus Christi, Texas. Peggy is a recognized authority in sea shells, this whole fascinating world having opened up to her as she coped with an ailing back. Swimming for health led to snorkeling, this to deep-sea diving, this to underwater photography, and this to a vast collection of exotic shells—collected through her own underwater explorations in seas and oceans all over the world.

Most shells are simply a part of the body of the creatures that grew them. They are intrinsic, inherent, and essential to the creature, as much so as are our skeletons to our bodies. Animals produce the shells, a vital part of their own bodies. We easily forget this when we see the countless shells on beaches, reefs, or as crushed materials for our roads.

Most ancient shells survive apart from the animals that grew them. Exceptions are such fossils as those of the Burgess Shale in Canada, remains of little animals that lived during the Cambrian Explosion almost a half-billion years ago and were discovered at the beginning of this century. Some such shells are so ordinary that we crush them under our feet or turn them into building materials. Some are indescribably beautiful, such as the Glory of the Seas.

Like these sea animals, churches build houses; but there is not and cannot be the same intrinsic relationship between a church and its house as there is between a sea shell and the animal that grew it. Churches build houses but do not grow them. Houses are not intrinsic to churches.

Hermit crabs illustrate another kind of relationship. We see these on almost any seashore, often countless and scurrying everywhere. Hermit crabs have their own intrinsic shells but also borrow or steal shells that they did not grow. They take cover in any suitable shell found unoccupied or from which they are able to evict the tenant. Hermit crabs make no investment in the borrowed or stolen shell. They make no commitment to it, ready to abandon it for a more suitable shell at any time. They find some convenience or security in the borrowed or stolen shell. Their detachment provides some measure of freedom for change of residence.

The ease with which a hermit crab may abandon one shell for a larger one serves the crab's need to grow. These crabs exercise no creativity as to the shells they occupy and put down no "roots" for the enrichment of their lives. Their whole relationship to the borrowed or stolen shell is self-serving.

Hermit crabs thus offer some positive analogies along with negatives as a paradigm for churches and church houses. For example, Mediterranean hermit crabs live with anemones in some expression of symbiosis. This principle of symbiosis is primary to any authentic church.

Spongicola is the name for tiny shrimp that find their home in a closed cylinder of a glass sponge known as Venus' Flower Basket, with the technical name *Euplectella*. Tiny shrimp known as *Spongicola* (sponge parasites) enter as pairs into this sponge (not a shell) before they are grown and remain there until they are too large to escape through the porous sponge. They mate and produce offspring, then die and remain entombed together inside the sponge. Skeletons of such glass sponges, with their pair of tiny dried shrimp imprisoned inside, are used as wedding gifts by the Japanese. The sponge is itself an animal that survives shelllike after its death.

In this relationship, the tiny shrimp contribute nothing to the sponge, but they do live, bear their young, and die within the sponge. Church houses may serve significantly in some parallel to what such sponges mean to tiny shrimp. The church must never earn the name of parasite.

Xenophora or Carrier Shells offer another paradigm for a church and its house. A Carrier Shell grows its own shell, then adds other shells and objects to its own shell. With its long snout, it carefully selects other shells and objects and cements them to its own shell. Sometimes the resultant complex is at least ten times larger than the original animal.

The intention of a carrier shell is not certain—whether all for show or to serve security purposes, frightening away predators. Its intention seems to be self-serving, whether aesthetic or protective; but at least it does carry others, albeit as passive objects and not as active subjects. Its name means "carrier of strangers," but it does not appear that its intention is to serve the shells or objects it carries.

The paradigm at least offers us a positive model of the church as carrier. It belongs to the church to be *Xenophora*, a carrier of strangers as well as those within the family.

Lessons for the Church as It Relates to Its Church House

As we this day celebrate the opening of this new house, let us not forget the basic distinction between Church and church house. Let this house never become an end in itself. Like the Church itself, its role is that of servanthood. It must never be worshiped, although it properly is a place of worship. Let not the monetary cost of erecting and maintaining buildings ever determine the character, direction, agenda, or priorities of Northminster Church. Let our prophetic voice never be muted for fear that budgetary funds may be jeopardized. Let us never forget that this house belongs to the Church, not the Church to the house.

On the positive side, let us rejoice in this beautiful and highly functional house, our first church house! Although we do not worship its beauty, its beauty helps us worship. Although all ground is holy ground and God can be worshiped anywhere, not just in Jerusalem or in Samaria (John 4:20f.), certain ground and certain houses can take on special meaning for us. Alex Haley has taught us well that "roots" do matter.

Let this be not only a special place for worship, but let it be a place for study, for fellowship, for recreation, and a base of operations for whatever service may be rendered to human beings near or far. Let this be a place where doors are open inclusively and not exclusively. Let these walls shelter us from walls designed to "segregate," that is, to separate God's flock (segregate is to set aside a *grex*, which means flock). Let this be a place where we so share our joys and sorrows, dreams and hopes, victories and failures, that it becomes holy ground for us and all who are willing to share with us.

Returning once more to the paradigm of shells, let us remember that a borrowed shell can shape or limit its occupant; but a living creature that grows its shell, shapes the shell to its own identity, needs, and mission. The proper function of a church house is not to shape or limit a church. It is proper for a church to shape its house, suited to its own identity, needs, and mission. So help us God!

10.
Wooden Tongues and Hungry Ears

Colossians 3:12-17

James E. Lamkin

(Though Northminster Church's new building was dedicated three weeks earlier, the church did not have its antique pulpit set in place until 29 September 1991. James E. Lamkin, a frequent preacher at Northminster during the early days of the church, spoke on this Sunday morning. Dr. Lamkin is the pastor of the Ravensworth Baptist Church in Annandale, Virginia.)

Acts of Wooden Altars: Speech, Service, and Song

I suppose that on the box in which all of these planks came was the label: "Some Assembly Required!" The stability of these boards came with considerable effort, I am sure. For these efforts, I am grateful, very grateful. It feels good.

Now, I hope no one was listening. It may have been embarrassing for both of us. Imagine overhearing a fellow talking to a piece of furniture. But I thought it only proper. I figure if you are going to talk *from* a pulpit, the least you can do is first talk *with* the pulpit. After all, from such a high perch, it and I are in this together—intimate strangers.

Earlier, while friends visited in the narthex, and the choir robed nearby, and while no one was listening, I slipped into the sanctuary. The pulpit and I had a visit. I found out it had a lot to say. But does that surprise you? After all, the pulpit is a talking piece of furniture.

You know how pulpits are. Just let there be a lull in the liturgy, and the pulpit will take over. It will simply start talking whether anybody is listening or not. Pulpits are like that: big mouths, most of them. Not all church furniture is so talkative, however.

Take the Table, for instance. The Table listens. The Table is the last remnant of the altar in Baptist churches. People get *altered* at the *altar*. We come with our sins, shames, and shortcomings. Sometimes the gravity of sin in my heart and the awaiting weight of the bread in my hand almost are too much. I approach the Table, head down, fearing to look up, lest the Table speak. It may say, "Not welcome, the body of Christ, *not* broken for you." I want to turn and walk away, lest I be turned away.

I risk a glance. Will the goblet come as grace or guilt? Out of the corner of my eye, the Table gestures. An invitation is signaled: "Come on," means the motion. "Come on, you too are welcome. The broken body is for you."

Some church furniture speaks, for instance pulpits. Other furniture such as the Table gestures. The organ neither motions nor talks; it sings. The organ sings and invites us to sing. What we are invited to sing cannot be said, for music takes up where words leave off. Even we who cannot sing are caught up in its power; we hear it singing for us. We theologians are left speechless before the commanding song of the organ, hands in our pockets, our dogma lifeless, our words flat.

So here we are, and here they are. Truly, all creation praises and preaches the glories of God—whether it be the grand song of the organ, the inviting silence of the Table, or the speech of the pulpit.

Since I cannot carry a tune in a bucket and am intimidated by silence, I turn most naturally with affection towards the pulpit—the talking pulpit. I bet you want to know what the two of us talked about before worship started.

"How was your trip across the ocean?" I asked.

"Okay," it replied, "didn't get wet once. Good thing too, because I'm allergic to water."

That worried me.

I thought I had better ease into the subject: "How do you like being in a . . . in a . . . Baptist church?"

"Baptist!" it said, startled. "Baptist?"

I did not know what would happen next. What a mess if the alarmed pulpit, recently transplanted, jumped and ran out of the sanctuary! If it had not been anchored to the chancel, I would have been more distraught.

"I'm Anglican," it replied with a dry British accent. "Episcopalian!" it said.

"Don't worry," said I. "Believe me, you'll feel at home at Northminster." (If I know pulpits, it does.)

The pulpit, the Table, the organ—these three pieces of furniture are the hat pegs of the sermon and worship. They remind us today, as they will every day, why we come to this place: to hear God and to be heard by God.

Talking Timbers

In the Baptist tradition, the pulpit is a symbol of the Word. Upon it, the Word rests. From it the Word is preached. Standing upon this piece of furniture, I am humbled to realize what it has heard: thousands of scriptures and millions of words over multiple decades. Dozens of preachers have climbed these steps. For over a century, anxious congregants watched in silence as pulpiteers carefully arranged notes on the lectern. Like world-class Scrabble players, they choreographed vowels and consonants in a chorus line searching for a creative order. The pulpit's cylindrical shape reminds us of a barrel, a cannon barrel, from which the Word of the Lord is hurled.

Listen closely. From its wooden memory come stories of fiery prophets voicing the relentless justice of God. Listen closely. Hear the whispers of weeping priests, their tears testifying of the measureless mercy of God.

Over three times my age, it is. We preachers who will speak from it would do well to listen to it before speaking. It reminds us of the Word. Its boards precede me and will succeed me. These planks prophesy to the Word's power.

From Paul's Pulpit Pen

We listen today to the pulpit pen of the Apostle Paul as he spoke to the Colossian Christians, folks whom he loved and grieved over and for whom he wanted freedom from heresy. Hear Paul: "Let the word of Christ dwell in you richly as you teach and admonish one another" (Col 3:16).

To read Paul is like watching only one end of a tennis match. We can only guess at what is happening on the net's other side. All scholars agree, however, that Paul felt the church was in danger of heresy. This "Colossian heresy" may have been an insistence on Jewish legalism, covered with a goodly layer of Gnostic philosophy. The first heresy separated from grace; the second heresy separated the Creator from the creation—a sour submarine sandwich kind of theology.

Thus, throughout the letter, Paul kept bringing them back to the center of faith, from which the church got its identity. The center, of course, was Jesus, the Word, the Christ.

"God's chosen ones, holy and dearly beloved" (3:12) he said, as if to transfer ownership of those words. Paul widened the strict Jewish definition of *chosen people*. He made it as wide as God. The outcast, the tax collector, the Gentile—all were God's people.

Paul reminded the Colossians first of identity, of who and whose they were. Then came the reminder that identity controls behavior. "Clothe yourselves with compassion, kindness, humility, meekness, and patience" (3:12). *Compassion* in the King James Version is translated "bowels of mercies," a mercy that rose from deep within. It is the same word Mark used when noting that Jesus felt compassion on the crowd for they were "as sheep without a shepherd" (6:32). It is also the same word Luke used when he described the waiting father's surprising response to the prodigal son's return and pictured the Good Samaritan's motivation when seeing the wounded man: compassion, deep compassion.

Paul said, "Clothe yourselves with love, which binds everything together" (3:14), a similar image to that of Ephesians 4:16, which speaks of "the whole body, joined and knit together . . . building itself up in love." *Knit together* is an odd verb. The image of a quilt comes to mind —various patches, sewn together by love, quilted.

Quilted in Christ

This summer, I met a young woman at Ridgecrest who was working on her doctorate. Her topic was: *Southern Baptist Convention Women in Pastoral Care, 1920-1965*. Her controlling metaphor for the dissertation was quilting. She and I swapped quilting stories. She told the best one, that of an older woman in a small community who made grief quilts.

The story goes that after a certain time following the death of a loved one, "the grief quilter" would offer her ministry to the widow or surviving family members. To their house she would go, stitching basket in hand. Some of the deceased person's clothes, now useless, would be cut into patches. As her hands sewed patch to patch, she listened to the story of grief, from beginning to ending: the couple's first meeting, their lives, their pains, their joys, their fights, their delights, their journey, the loss. Since neither quilts nor grief are worked through overnight, the process took a graceful while. In the end, the result was a quilt: constructed, beautiful, warm, comforting, made of memories, patched together. It made hope.

Most of us here this morning are adults. We can say things out loud, even our pain and shame. I think you can stand it. We all remember that the formation of this church family, and eventually this building, came out of your collective sadness, your grief and loss. Having lost one family, you formed a new one.

You, we, are like a bunch of patches. Patches of grief and hope stitched by the needle of the Spirit and by the threads of word, song, and prayer. You have been knitted together, quilted, into a new church.

My roots come from Bienville Parish, Louisiana, where they used to have quilting parties. Maybe you have been to one. Each participant brought some pieces of fabric, a needle, and some thread. Those who did not know how to quilt were taught. Persons who knew how stitched with seasoned hands and gossiped with eager mouths. Through the process, they had community. In the end, they had a quilt.

This building has been the result of a quilting party, from design to decor, from floors to financing—patches all—some small, some large, knitted together, and most of the time . . . in love.

There is much nourishment in this Colossian text, more food than a twenty-minute-sermon sized plate can hold. On another day, there is more to say about the text's forgiveness words, but that is the message of the Table. On another day, there is more to say about the text's mention of singing psalms, hymns, and spiritual songs—but not today; that is the domain of the organ.

On this day, we highlight other words and the pulpit on which they rest: "Let the *word* of Christ dwell in you richly." In addition, we celebrate the approaching completion of the quilting party as you take your place among other high, arched roofs and stained glass sanctuaries in this town—a congregation of Christ's people quilted together in love.

As Paul did for the Colossian Christians, I do for you. I remind you of who and whose you are. Indeed, the Northminster quilt holds painful/hopeful memories made beautiful. The Northminster quilt holds loving/caring warmth, offering welcome to cold strangers in search of family.

This quilted community will not be a church of the easy answer. Those looking for quick explanations may have trouble finding them here. But for those seeking the comfort and discomfort of mystery—the mystery of God and the mystery of humankind—for those seeking a place to explore where these mysteries both collide and connect, then the beauty and warmth of this quilt is offered.

Calvin Miller said,

> When a potential member visits a church, he or she comes again only
> if that church is in touch with the world they hunger for, not the one
> where they live.[1]

Of that world, this pulpit reminds us. From that world, this Table calls us. To that world, the organ carries us. Through them all, and to this place, we come weekly and weakly, listening once again for the old story —the old, old story of Jesus and his love. Amen.

Endnote

[1]Calvin Miller, *Spirit, Word, and Story* (Waco: Word Books, 1989) 20.

V.
Hurting

"Remember that you were a slave in the land of Egypt."
(Deut 24:22)

"Beloved, do not be surprised at the fiery ordeal that is taking place among you to test you, as though something strange were happening to you."

(1 Peter 4:12)

Hurt was a constant companion to members of Northminster Church throughout the early days of their pilgrimage. The religion-inflicted wounds, spiritual bruises, and emotional pains that marked the people who first met together, before anyone dared to express the hope of forming a new church, did not immediately disappear once a commitment to ministry through the establishment of Northminster Church was made. In fact, new problems emerged, and additional hurts demanded attention.

Some members had more difficulty putting the past behind them than others. One man, who grieved very little over past losses, explained that he had been ready to get on with something new for a long time. He was far more excited about the future than upset because of the past. Another gentleman, also possessed by a genuine excitement about the future, admitted, "I could't go back, but it was hard to leave." A long-time member of another church felt great sadness over the many friends she was leaving behind as she started a new segment of her spiritual journey. By way of contrast, though, one of her close friends at Northminster declared, "I didn't feel like I belonged anywhere." Obviously, this woman also felt pain, but it was a different kind.

The individuals for whom the new venture was most difficult were those leaving family members in other congregations. One woman described her parents' difficulties with her family's involvement in Northminster: "We were the black sheep of the family."

In some instances, anxieties about the future compounded family-related pains centered in other churches. Connie and Russell Smallwood worried about their seven-year-old twin daughters. Connie explains that she knew the decision to be a part of this new church was right for her, but she feared her daughters would lose something. At one point during the congregation's first year, Connie and Russell talked with their daughters about moving to a church in which they could be a part of a larger group of young people. Both Laura and Leslie protested such a move, "But this is our church!" The congregation had made every person in it to feel a part of its mission, and the Smallwood twins were not about to relinquish their sense of responsibility or joy.

Sources of people's hurt varied, as did the reasons for and expressions of their hurt, but hurt itself was a nonvariable. Virtually every individual in the initial fellowship of Northminster Church knew the reality of hurt intimately. Indeed, the small band of faithful people that set its sights on answering God's call to form a church constituted a community of pain, not at all an unusual characterization or identity for the people of God.

Even on occasions of joyous celebration, a residue of hurt tied to the past often tugged at people's hearts. The Palm Sunday on which members of Northminster signed the church's charter was such a day. No one had offered more encouragement or worked harder toward this moment than Don and Cathe Nixon. Because the husband and wife ministers were on a paid leave of absence from another congregation (a leave from which they were not expected to return, but a leave the church had promised to discontinue if the Nixons accepted a position with another congregation), they could not sign the charter along with other members of their spiritual family. As fifty-five Northminster people penned their names on the charter of the church one by one, Don and Cathe grieved, Don sitting on a piano bench weeping openly and uncontrollably. Thoughtfully, the newly-formed church voted to keep its charter open until later in the spring when Don and Cathe could sign it. By that time, thirty additional people also had signed the charter.

A major source of hurt for people in Northminster Church was the reaction of the Baptist community to their establishment of this new church. While looking for a meeting place in their earliest days together, the congregation faced rejection and opposition from more than one Baptist body. One member recalls, "Not a single Baptist church in town was supportive of our efforts."

Reactions to Northminster Church in the Baptist community of Monroe did not mirror reactions within the larger community, either religious or secular, of Monroe. Northminster's vision, enthusiasm, programs, and ministries received bountiful amounts of affirmation and encouragement from other church fellowships in Monroe as well as from innumerable community organizations and local leaders and many Baptist bodies outside the city.

Northminster Church sought to be a cooperative fellowship working with other Baptists in the Northeast Louisiana Baptist Association and the Louisiana Baptist Convention, though immediately after its formation, the executive officer of the state convention asked one of its members to resign from his position on the executive board of the Louisiana Baptist Convention. The church applied for membership in the local Baptist association, having allocated funds for both the association and the state convention in its very first budget.

The Northeast Louisiana Baptist Association provisionally accepted Northminster Church for one year, assigning the church "watchcare" status within the association. Then, the missions committee of the association, employing a process never before utilized in responding to a church's request to join the association, asked the Northminster congregation to answer a series of questions. The committee indicated that these answers would be evaluated, and then the appropriateness of the church's membership in the association would be determined.

Several Baptist leaders who reviewed the list of questions presented to Northminster Church by the associational committee expressed dismay at their substance. Among numerous other inquiries related to doctrinal matters, the associational committee asked: Who do you believe Jesus is? Do you believe that he was human? Do you support in both faith and practice the 1963 Baptist Faith and Message Statement? Do you interpret this to mean that all of the Bible is inspired and without any mixture of error? Can a person be a member of Northminster Church without personally repenting of sin and placing his faith in Jesus as Savior and Lord? Do you believe and teach the doctrine of once saved, always saved?

Questions related to "informational matters" were far more extensive. The church was asked to explain why it had no deacons and no pastor, and whether or not, if this changed in the future, "a woman may be ordained or called as pastor." Information was requested about how policies and financial decisions were made in the church without deacons and a pastor. The committee found problematic the church's identification of itself as "non-sexist," "non-exclusive," and "ecumenical." Questions were raised as to whether or not the church was unwilling to accept pastoral authority and why the church continued to have pulpit speakers who were not Baptists.

Many old feelings of distrust, suspicion, hurt, and anger resurfaced in the Northminster congregation when the association's two pages of questions were received. The church used what could have been a bad moment in an overwhelmingly positive manner, however.

A decision was made that no one person or no small committee would speak for the church in response to these inquiries. Rather, the church members resolved to discuss together the questions one by one.

Members of Northminster saw this challenge from the association as an opportunity to further refine their beliefs and define their identity. So, as a congregation, Northminster Church developed a confession of faith to share with the local association in response to its inquiries.

When members of the Northminster congregation met with members of the associational committee to respond to the committee's questions, a frank discussion ensued. In preliminary remarks, Craig Henry said to the committee,

> We hope you have not prejudged us. . . . We must honestly say that we are hurt and saddened that none of you has ever visited our services of worship and sought to have dialogue with us to help discover who we are.

Craig identified the church as a diverse group of men and women: teachers, engineers, homemakers, doctors, plumbers, counselors, artists, contractors, . . . three ordained Baptist ministers, . . . eleven ordained as deacons by other Baptist churches.

Then he characterized the church's beliefs:

> We hold strongly to our Baptist heritage of freedom of conscience, the priesthood of all believers, and soul competency. We believe that Christ came to free us from a system of religious legalism, not to burden us with another meaningless system.

Line by line, Northminster members responded to each of the examining committee's questions. Apparently most objectionable to the committee were the church's openness to the reception of members having experienced meaningful baptism in another denomination, its affirmation of the ordination of women, and its lack of readiness to call a pastor.

After speaking at length of his Baptist heritage and loyalties, Harold Hughens explained why the word "Baptist" is not used on the church's signage and in its publicity:

> We do feel that the name Baptist has received some negative press over the political battles going on in our denomination. There has developed an exclusive spirit among some Baptists. We do not want people to

conclude that we are exclusive, and that they are not welcome in our services, because of the misunderstanding of who we Baptists are.

Eventually Northminster members received a letter informing them that the examining committee had decided not to recommend to the association that Northminster Church be accepted into its fellowship. Rejection. Again! A potential source of additional hurt. Northminster members responded to this decision gracefully, however. One man explained that he considered it an honor for the church to be excluded from this fellowship on the basis of doctrine.

A bounty of positive factors emerged from the church's involvement in this particular controversy. The director of missions in the association, Jerry Edmondson, and some members of the missions committee voiced positive, supportive comments about this new church in Monroe. Most importantly, though, Northminster Church had been forced to hammer out its theology. How many local churches do that, or even have an opportunity to do that? Diversity did not hinder the development of confessions around which the church found unanimity. Through scriptural investigations, honest dialogue, and the interaction of various personal opinions, Northminster Church came to know its beliefs and identity better than ever—and the people of Northminster liked what they knew.

Not uncommonly, a strong bond develops between people who have endured hardships and shared hurts with each other. That certainly was the case with members of Northminster Church. Kay Southern articulated what virtually every member of the congregation felt: "We have shared so many hurts. I could call any member at 3:00 A.M., and they would come." Care-giving was not limited to members of the church, though.

Knowing full well the dynamics of rejection, hurt, and displacement, Northminster Church became a fellowship especially sensitive and open to people who had been rejected, hurt, and displaced elsewhere. Joyce Loftin mused, "I don't believe in excluding anyone. . . . If God didn't exclude me, why shouldn't I welcome everybody?" As so often happens under the leadership of God, a congregation of people who knew the depths of hurt became a congregation of healers ready to extend its ministry to all who hurt.

Citing a statement from Kennon L. Callahan while speaking to the examining committee of the local association, Craig Henry beautifully described the "wounded-healers" nature of this congregation. Craig pointed out that a person discovers real community where people are joined together in a covenant that causes reconciliation, wholeness, caring, and justice to take place. Then he said, "Under God's leadership, in the name of Jesus Christ, that is the kind of church we are committed to being in our world."

11.
Life Together

Nancy Hastings Sehested

(After leading Northminster Church in a weekend study on spirituality, Nancy Hastings Sehested preached in the morning worship service on 7 February 1993. Rev. Sehested lives in Memphis, Tennessee, where she is the pastor of Prescott Memorial Baptist Church.)

You have revived my soul, walking among such a vibrant, alive, imaginative, and caring community of faith. In these troubled times, it is good to have companions for the journey. You give me hope. I will carry the hope of knowing that God has planted God's people everywhere. Keep shining on! You are indeed part of God's light.

As the preacher among you today, I come to announce what is already taking place among you. It is a word that you are living in your life together. I have come to remind you what you already know: Life together in Christ costs. Our life together with our spouses, children, family members, church family members, and community is all related to our life together in Christ.

We have mercifully come to the end of a year of constant campaigning. You might recall how candidates were trying to outdo each other on "family values." God knows we could certainly use such, alongside some government values and business values. Today we are looking at life together, life in relationship—family values, so to speak. What better place to start than with the Bible.

We can start from the very beginning with the first family, Adam and Eve. Things started out pretty good. As a matter of fact, all of their life was marked by God as "good." Just east of Eden, trouble started in paradise. Communication problems developed between them.

God was called in as a marriage counselor. It was the classic blaming-the-other-person couple problem: Eve said: "Well, he said . . ." Adam said: "Well, she said . . ." He said. She said. Blame. Blame. Blame. God blamed them both. Then God cut the conversation short and sent them to work in the garden.

Then, I guess you heard about their children. They knocked Adam and Eve out of the running for any parenting award. The sibling rivalry between Cain and Abel was intense. Cain killed his brother.

Now, how do you account for this? If I were God, and I was writing a handbook on how to have a good life together and promote good strong family values, I would have written about the model family—for example, Ozzie and Harriet. But right at the very beginning, the first family blew it. Can you make some sense out of this?

Where are the biblical models for life together? Abraham had a mistress. Isaac's wife Rebecca was scheming and conniving, playing favorites with her sons. Did Moses consult his wife Zipporah before agreeing to lead a mission trip through the desert? Ruth did not save herself before her marriage to Boaz. The good shepherd King David murdered a man to take his wife, Bathsheba. King Solomon married 700 princesses and had 300 concubines. I hope Jeremiah never married. His wife would not have had a moment's peace with his mouth always getting him into trouble. Their house would have been picketed. God told Hosea to marry a prostitute named Gomer. God's premarital counseling was, "Go and get married to this harlot. She will be unfaithful, and your children will be just like her." Sure puts a bounce in a groom's step to hear reassuring words like that!

Those were all Old Testament couples, though. Surely the New Testament provides us with some good role models of life together in marital bliss. Mary and Joseph got off to a rough start with Joseph trying to duck out of the engagement when Mary turned up pregnant. Jesus never married—good thing. Can you imagine being married to someone so perfect? (My husband has such a hard time.) Jesus had no kids and ignored his mother from time to time. Paul never married. He even strongly advised against it. So, who does that leave? I nominate Priscilla and Aquilla. We know so little about them that I suppose it is safe to idealize them.

What about life together in the congregation? Moses led a congregation full of cantankerous and grumpy people through the wilderness. Jeremiah preached to a picky congregation that thought his messages should stay upbeat and peppy, and when they were not, the people were ready to put him in the stocks.

What about the early church and its life together? What a mess—quarreling and divisions! I guess you heard about the couple who lied and dropped dead in the sanctuary. The early church had a mess of a time agreeing on hymn selection and whether to stand, sit, or kneel for communion.

Why did God not make sure that the perfect example of the perfect church was recorded in the Bible? The way I figure it is this: If God can sweep through the lives of the nuts people in the Bible and transform their hearts and use them for God's purposes, then there is hope. Maybe God will keep doing the same with nuts people like us too.

Face it. It is very difficult to find some models for a life together. What does life together in mutual love and respect look like? The Bible gives us some good clues—clues, that's all, my friends. God respects our freedom so much that God does not give us blueprints or exact measures. God gives clues, startling and surprising clues at that.

In Luke 14, Jesus said, "If you want to follow me . . ." Jesus was saying that the road of discipleship costs. Count the cost. Before you build a tower, check to make sure you can afford to finish it. An unfinished tower will make you a laughing stock of the community. A king has to know his military power before marching against the enemy. Use common sense. A couple calculates if they can afford the mortgage payments. Count the cost. Plan ahead. You had to decide about plans for this building and taking up the offering.

So, what does this have to do with life together, in love and in discipleship? Everything. Is this not contrary to Jesus' other teachings? Jesus taught and lived a love offered freely, spontaneously, passionately—one that did not count the cost. Forgive seven times? No, seventy times seven! If you are forced to go one mile, go two. Turn the other cheek. Do not worry about tomorrow, what you shall eat and wear. Consider the lilies. Love your enemies. Wine running low at the wedding feast? Here, swim in it! Having a banquet? Invite the lame, the blind, and bring them in.

Jesus lived a life of loving abandon. He loved everyone and anyone: prostitutes, beggars, lepers, and low-life tax collectors. Jesus was the "pied piper" of love, drawing crowds to him with his generous, uncautious, never-counting-the-cost kind of love.

Is this not what first drew us to Jesus Christ as well? Unconditional love! Freeing love! Is this not the miracle of the grace we have known through the spirit of Christ—a free, uncalculating expression of love? Is this not the gospel—the not-counting-the-cost heart of Christian love?

So, what is this business about counting the cost? Why did Jesus put this in? Jesus said you do not want to start a tower and not be able to finish it. Count the cost. But is it not better to have loved and lost than never to have loved at all?

Now I cannot be sure about this, but I have an idea about why Jesus told these parables. He was talking about our life together as disciples. He was surely aware that we can be tempted to romanticize the journey and think all will be happy and joyous and freeing.

Jesus knew that we are always tempted to register our feelings on the emotional chart several times a day, and if we do not feel good, success-ful, or deliriously happy, then we might be tempted to quit. Give up. Forget this life together stuff; it is too hard.

Remember Jesus' words to the woman along the roadside who was carried away by her emotions. She yelled out to Jesus, "How blessed for a mother to have a son like you!" Could Jesus not have responded with, "You are right. I have a terrific mother." Instead, he tossed away her compliment with the words, "Yes, rather, blessed are they who hear the word of God and keep it."

Jesus was counting the cost. He knew it had cost Mary dearly to have a son such as him, like a sword piercing through her soul. Jesus seemed to be saying that good feelings and good intentions will not build God's kingdom of love. If you just want a warm, fuzzy feeling of unconditional positive regard, stay off the path of discipleship; this path will cost you.

Think of the cost of racial reconciliation. The tower has become far more complicated to build than we ever imagined. Jesus reminded us that if we are going to live by God's kingdom values, then our world will be turned inside out and upside down. Our old patterns of relating to our husband or wife, brothers and sisters, children, neighbors, and co-workers will not work anymore. We are living and loving by God's priorities, and that starts with our deepest and most intimate relationships. Life together with God means that life together with human beings will not be shaped by God's housekeeping rules, and it costs.

Some of you know my husband Ken. We were ordained together and live our lives as co-partners in mission. (Ken is the director of the Baptist Peace Fellowship of North America.) We have been married twenty years.

When Ken and I became parents, we were ecstatic with joy. Our feel-ings were soaring with delight. Our commitment to mutually caring for our new baby was no problem to achieve. Our feelings carried us on the wings of our promise to both take equal responsibility for the care and nurture of our child, but the weeks wore on. Sleepless nights left us both a bit tired and cranky. Seven days a week, twenty-four hours a day, we were responsible. This blessed bundle of joy had some times of feeling like a burden.

Then subtly, tiptoeing into our minds was resentment. We started keeping an internal record of who was the last one to change the dirty diaper and whose turn was next. I was convinced I changed more diapers than he did. He insisted he had done his fair share. What happened to the good 'ole days when this was woman's work? We would not have had this problem if we had stuck to our assigned societal roles! But, oh no, we had to have this vision, this commitment to both caring for our child, to mutual parenting. It cost.

So, what did we do? We made a chart to help get through those times when we did not feel like changing diapers. We charted times when each of us was fully attentive to the baby's needs. We placed the chart on the refrigerator. This instantly eliminated the inner record book of growing resentments. Justice was served; it was merciful for the whole family, but it cost. It still does. You should know.

It is costly to negotiate, schedule, and plan—so that our children have the nurture and care of both parents on a day-to-day basis, especially when most of us have a work world that does not encourage this commitment but works against family values. It takes a while for our visions to take hold in the depths of our being, where real transformation takes place. Sometimes we have to practice our way into our vision of equality and justice before it becomes second nature to us. It costs.

Think of the cost you have paid in stepping out for freedom and truth. Think of the cost you have known in breaking with ties that had meant so much to you. You have paid a price in building this Baptist tower of the priesthood of the believer and autonomy of the local church and soul competency.

Your life together in Christ has come at a cost. Some of you have even had to leave your father, mother, brothers, and sisters to step out for God's truth—to be true to your call to discipleship. You know what it is to bear the cross of Christ.

In the Christian marriage ceremony, we do not promise our feelings of love; we promise our faithfulness. When the Bible brings up the understanding of love—the Bible is clear that it is not the feeling of love —it is not how many times you say, "I love you." The word always used is *hesed* ("faithfulness"). In the New Testament, it is *hesed*, the faithfulness of love even unto death.

With friends, we all know that the ones we are most grateful for are the faithful ones through the griefs and sufferings. They are the ones who do more than mean well.

As a church, you are off to a flaming good start in building a life together in love. It is built with bricks of justice, but mercy dwells within. It costs.

None of us will build a perfect marriage anymore than we will build a perfect family, a perfect self, or a perfect church. God forbid that we should strive for it. Our life together is not an object to be formed; it is a life to be lived. The truth is, none of us would enter life together if we really knew the cost.

Finally, through all the cost and confusion, through all the tragedy and beauty and mystery of our life together, it is God's faithfulness— God's faithfulness of love even unto death—that grants us the grace to carry on and carry through.

Brothers and sisters in Christ, in your life together as the part of the body of Christ called Northminster, may you continue to dream God's dreams for you and the world. May you continue to bless the baffled and caress the grieving. May you continue to grant courage and a megaphone to the pushed-down and the pushed-aside. May you do all you can to halt the hell-raisers of war and violence and hunger. May you give extra helpings of hope to our young, tickle with good humor our old, and lighten the load of our in-betweens. May God continue to give us all some real good clues as to what love looks like with skin on. In the name of the one who was made flesh and whose Spirit dwells among us—Jesus the Christ, our brother. Amen.

VI.
Celebrating

"Not one of all the good promises that the Lord had made to the house of Israel had failed; all came to pass."

(Josh 21:45)

"Rejoice in the Lord always; again, I will say, rejoice."
(Phil 4:4)

"Therefore, let us celebrate the festival, not with the old yeast, the yeast of malice and evil, but with the unleavened bread of sincerity and truth."
(1 Cor 5:8)

Everything had gone so well in the development of their young church that members of Northminster were very hesitant to initiate the process of calling a pastor. "Why take such a risk when all was well?" one young man asked. Several factors fed the hesitation. Negatively, most of the people in this congregation had not had good experiences with a pastor-led church. A leader in the church admitted, "I have never had a pastor I liked or trusted." Positively, the church family wanted a staff of "enabling ministers" rather than an administrative hierarchy with a pastor at the top. Church members had learned that without a pastor they did a lot more of what church members should do in terms of ministry, and they did not want this to stop.

Another factor in the congregation's reticence to begin a search for a pastor was a concern for the feelings of the two staff members who had been with the church since its earliest days: Don and Cathe Nixon. Each of these individuals strongly resisted any organizational rearrangement that would reduce the freedom with which they functioned or the level of ministry that they enjoyed and have them "serving under a pastor." Both wanted a pastoral colleague, but not a "boss." Members of the church realized the potential difficulties of securing a pastor comfortable with this arrangement. No one wanted to call a pastor who would seek to radically reorganize the church or who would only stay with the church briefly. The staff and congregation were too fragile to go through such conflict.

For an extended period of time, calling a pastor was not a major concern. The church could not afford a pastor. Besides, most worshipers enjoyed the variety of pulpit guests who came to Northminster regularly. Don and Cathe Nixon were taking care of the ministry needs of the congregation that were not being met by church members themselves. Almost everyone was comfortable with this situation.

With the passing of time, however, especially after their move into the new building, members of the congregation began to express a need for more continuity in the pulpit. Alongside several people who continued to feel the church did not need a pastor were individuals who felt the church would not really get on with its ministry until it called a pastor. One woman kept saying, "We need a pastor. A pastor would mean we are going to be here." Additionally, the Nixons were rapidly becoming overworked and ready for assistance.

Once more the church was forced to make a major decision before it was ready. A person who had been extremely well received by the congregation as a frequent worship leader-preacher presented himself to the church as a candidate for its pastor. Some members were eager to secure the services of this man immediately. Others, though, had reservations about moving so quickly.

Not too long after the church voted to request the coordinating committee to try to work out the arrangements by which this man could be named pastor, differences of opinion surfaced regarding worship leadership and administrative philosophy. Though finally the church settled on using the name of pastor for the person to be called, careful consideration was given to other titles for this position, such as minister of proclamation. After church members expressed their views about the role of a pastor and drew up a job description for the pastor, the man who had expressed a strong interest in the position withdrew his name from consideration by the church.

Again avoiding what could have been a difficult, if not traumatic, situation, the church moved to establish a process by which a pastor would be called. From a list of names suggested by the coordinating committee, church members chose a pastor search committee made up of four women and four men and ordered that the two current staff members along with the chair of the coordinating council, Tom Stricklin, serve as ex officio members of that committee.

Still with no desire to move quickly toward a consideration of specific candidates, the pastor search committee requested the church to describe the kind of pastor it wanted. Responses from the congregation helped the committee to see the church's need for a pastor earlier than would have been the case otherwise.

Members of the Northminster congregation made their wills known about the kind of pastor desired, but refused to impose any restrictions on the pastor search committee or to develop any specific instructions for it. The search committee was free to look at candidates without regard for their gender or denominational affiliation. All wanted "the right person."

A Personal Word

My first contact with Northminster Church came in the spring of 1992 by way of a letter from the congregation's pastor search committee. That piece of correspondence (mailed to several other people as well) inquired about the possibility of my interest in serving as the church's first pastor. At that particular time in my own spiritual pilgrimage, I was not at all sure that I ever wanted to attend a church regularly again much less pastor a church filled with people I had never met. Friends whose opinions I trust, however, especially Walter (Buddy) Shurden, encouraged me to respond positively. So, I did.

When I received a list of questions that the pastor search committee wanted me to answer, I was intrigued. No search committee had ever asked me these types of questions before. Still fresh in my memory was the repulsive question raised by the chair of a pastor search committee from another congregation in our first formal conversation together: "What will it take to get you?" The people from Northminster requested that I write to them about my spiritual heroes, the authors I most often read, the events that have shaped my life, and my vision of the church's mission to the local community as well as more theologically-oriented subjects. I sensed something special, if not unique, about these folks.

After several months of correspondence and telephone conversations, my wife Judy and I met most of the members of the Northminster congregation. Frankly, our first weekend together was more like an extended homecoming party than an interview or a "trial sermon weekend." We bonded quickly. Subsequently, we have bonded deeply.

My first Sunday in worship as the pastor of Northminster Church was the first Sunday of Advent in 1992. The scheduling was no accident. The congregation's unanimous vote to invite Judy and me to join their fellowship occurred on the last Sunday evening prior to Advent. However, many of the people felt it important that we begin our spiritual journey together at the beginning of a season of riotous hope and holy promise.

The worship service in which I was formally installed as Northminster Church's pastor took place on a Sunday afternoon about six weeks later. Don Nixon spoke to the congregation about this occasion:

> For all of us that make up this family called Northminster, the unraveling of this moment is nothing short of a miracle of God. The journey

. . . the struggle . . . the paths that have led us to this day have not always been the safest or the most accepted or the easiest to walk. Along the way many of us have stumbled, and some have even fallen, but that was never the defeat, because we did not journey in darkness but rather walked blindly by the unquestioned light of God's guidance.

There is no question that this little band of dirty, blemished, strugglers have set out on an adventuresome journey and that without the determination and dedication to that inner call one of the greatest experiences of this life could have been missed. When the world called them foolish, their God was calling them to new heights, and now they have paused in travel to make welcome another sojourner among the ranks.

During this service, the congregation sang for the first time "Alleluia! Sing Te Deum Laudamus!" a hymn that D. H. Clark wrote for this occasion. D. H. explains,

The hymn is a poetic rendering of the prayer of thanksgiving offered by the people of Northminster Church on Thanksgiving Day, 1992. Don Nixon asked that all church members enumerate their blessings for which they were particularly thankful at that momentous time in the life of the church. That was the time we had received the joyous news that Dr. C. Welton Gaddy had accepted the call to become Northminster's first pastor. *Te Deum laudamus* is the beginning of an early Latin hymn that expresses the Christian outpouring of praise to God. The hymn tune "Northminster Te Deum" is based on the plainchant melody that was the original tune used for the hymn in the medieval church.

The young people of Northminster presented the new pastor with several symbolic gifts from the congregation—"things that must be packed for you to carry as we start out on this new day." In his words describing the nature of these gifts, Don Nixon conveyed fundamental insights into the essential nature of this fellowship.

First came a Bible:

This is the Word of the Lord . . . our direction for the journey. As we walk, we need your understanding interpreting among us, and we need you to discover with us its meaning in today's experiences. Be among us as a devoted searcher for truth and a courageous adventuresome guide in the quest for freedom.

Next I received a pot filled with water:

This vessel contains water. For generations water has been a symbol for the people of God—for deliverance and for the crossing over into new . . . beginnings. Carry it as a reminder of obedience and deliverance. Carry it, for along the way we will discover people who need to wash and feel clean.

A flask of oil was set in my hands:

There is oil . . . for on any journey it is inevitable that pain, strife, disease, and opposition will be the enemy. So be among us as a healer and as a reconciler.

The final gift almost took my breath away. Every member of every family in the congregation had selected a swatch of fabric that carried great personal meaning to that individual. Then, Mary Sandow expertly and exquisitely brought these diverse pieces of material together in a magnificent stoll. As the stoll was placed around my neck, I heard the words:

You will have the honor of wearing the vestment of distinction. It is not made of the finest spun linen or of the rarest threads available. It is a tapestry carefully, originally, and uniquely designed for this day. The individual fabrics were brought as an offering from each person within our family and reflect to you who they are. As you wear it, be reminded that the spirits of each of us go with you, offering strength and hope and pride wherever and whenever you choose to wear it. Be a priest among us—assuring us of forgiveness, calling us to maturity, and challenging us to a life of service.

After I was equipped for travel, the people said their prayers for the new pastor. Penny Joiner prayed,

May he sense an unconditional love that accepts, forgives, and challenges his leadership.

George Brian prayed,

> May he offer guidance and growth for a community of inclusiveness .
> . . and . . . reflect to each of us the life that echoes "a servant to all."

Janie Fuchs prayed,

> May he find peace, fulfillment, and a deepened spiritual relationship
> with God through the support, understanding, and dedicated service of
> the people for whom he has been called to serve.

Peggy Underwood prayed,

> May he be the leader of expanded visions revealing the truth, not in
> limited interpretations of yesterdays, but in understandings that are vital
> for this time and place.

Susan Curry prayed,

> May he find in us friendship.

Late that evening, as members of the church and members of my
family sat together in Kay Southern's living room (the place where it all
began) eating pizza and reflecting on the day, I had the joy, on behalf of
the congregation, of presenting to Don Nixon a stoll, exactly like the one
I received. Members of the church had thoughtfully prepared this vestment for him. Then, for hours, hearts warmed, smiles appeared, spirits
glowed, and tears flowed as various people in the fellowship shared their
memories of the church's pilgrimage.

Blessing Others

As I continue to listen to members of Northminster Church reflect on
their experiences related to forming a congregation, I hear only two re-
grets. One is that the church formed amid a great deal of hurt caused by
severed relationships within other churches, one in particular. Most people who voice this regret hasten to add, though, that they cannot imagine
how they would have found the courage to start such an ambitious pilgrimage unless they had been forced to do so.

A second regret, which I hear more frequently and from far more people, is that they waited so long before starting a new church. Time and time again, individuals say of Northminster Church, "I am so sorry I missed such a church as this for so much of my life."

When it comes to starting a new church, difficulties are inevitable. Controversy goes with the territory. Financial needs outrun monetary resources. But, it can be done, and it is worth doing. One member of Northminster Church speaks of never again wanting to be a part of a church in which if someone sees a need, he or she waits for someone else to take care of it rather than meeting it. The people in this church have found great pleasure in performing menial tasks for the good of the fellowship: an interior designer cleaning the bathrooms, an engineer taking out the garbage, a lawyer vacuming the Sunday School rooms, an opthamologist washing windows, a professor rearranging tables and chairs, and on and on the story goes.

An older lady says of the church, "It has been a surprise every day." Her best friend declares, "The surprise is that we have come this far; the blessing it has been!" A young man admits, "Sometimes I just walk into this church building and tears come to my eyes." An older gentleman says, "I've never felt freedom like this; this has been the most exciting part of my life." A university professor agrees with this last statement and adds, "As an adult, I have never felt such love as I have here."

With her usual candor, Hannah Clark articulates what many others think to themselves: "I've been surprised I love this church so much, that it means so much to me. I never knew I could have this level of commitment to a church. Before, no church meant much to me, and I didn't mean much to any church."

Members of Northminster Church frequently speak compassionately and hopefully of individuals who have dropped out of a church or who are members of congregations in which they feel dissatisfied and trapped. As one lady related to me the history of her involvement in Northminster Church, she said, "I want everybody to have this." Similarly, Dibble Pate declared, "If all these people who are hurting could just see, they could do it!" Tom Stricklin added, "You do a disservice to yourself and to your own conscience unless you do."

Wishes become works as words become deeds. Northminster members speak, work, and give to help other people who are beginning to form new congregations. Hannah Clark is very directive: "If you can find two friends, start a new church. You don't have to have great resources. Stay fixed on worship, and let all else fall in place around that."

Often I ask people who have been in Northminster since its inception if they would have done anything differently along the way. In response to that question, Tom Stricklin confesses,

> We were so close to one another and trying to do what we thought was best for us and the community . . . I don't know what we could have done differently. We made mistakes, but none large enough to impede our progress.

Seldom is the answer to that inquiry anything but "no." When I posed this question to Harold Hughens, however, he responded with words that best place the whole pilgrimage in a proper perspective: "I can't think of a thing I would do differently. You can't change miracles!"

12.
Sketching a Vision

Isaiah 40:1-5
Matthew 16:13-18
Galatians 5:22-6:2

C. Welton Gaddy

(I preached this sermon on 15 November 1992, at the invitation of the Northminster pastor search committee.)

The sermon for this morning consists of a personal confession that developed while poking around in the holy scriptures in search of a vision, a vision to be commended to the Northminster congregation. What I have to say is set against a backdrop of pictures—a collage of images—and spoken amid a cocaphany of sounds, some holy and many not holy at all.

I hear Almighty God saying, "Comfort, comfort my people."

I see the Messiah turning over this challenge along with his work of redemption to a bunch of failures.

I see valley after valley filled with dry bones. I hear—at least, I think I hear—the rustling of *ruach*, the Spirit of God, who can bring warm flesh, pulsating blood, and meaningful activity to those considered dead.

I see people with all kinds of problems as well as promise, griefs intermingled with joys, doubts in heated dialogue with faith. I hear Paul, a spokesperson for God, say, "You are the body of Christ."

I see frustration and anger directed toward the institutional church. But I hear the Lord of the church talking about a fellowship in which all people are welcome, mercy is preeminent, and a nonstop party is underway celebrating the reality of redemption.

I see a world of hungry people—some hungry for food, some malnourished from a lack of love, some ravenously desirous of friendship, some starving for grace. I hear Jesus say, "Feed my sheep."

One day in Nairobi, Kenya, truth sneaked up on me in such a manner that only later did I realize the force with which it had hit me. A friend from South Africa closed a meeting with a prayer of benediction. He began by saying, "We thank you God for the privilege of bearing one another's burdens and thus fulfilling the law of Christ." I do not know how the prayer ended. I was not listening.

I knew well the inspiration for this man's words, Galatians 6:2, but never before had I really connected the bearing of other people's burdens with obedience to the law of Christ. For me, law meant prohibitions and additional burdens, not liberation and weight-eradicating love. I certainly had not considered shouldering someone else's difficulties as a privilege for which to be thankful.

The longer the opening sentence of that benediction resounded in my psyche, though, the more I began to feel that it captured the essence of Christian fellowship, the basic work of the church, and an unmistakeable sign of people who have sold out to the gospel. Looking at faith from this perspective, various components of my faith began to make more sense than ever before.

The gospel really is good news. That may sound to you like no great discovery, but I had lived most of my life with people who seemed to feel an obligation to make the gospel bad news. They could make a promise sound like a threat, twist an invitation to life until it became a condemnation to death, and see danger behind every experience of joy. Sad. The gospel is good news.

Only when I understand the gospel in a manner that makes me want to say, "That's hard to believe" or "That's too good to be true," have I really begun to understand the gospel at all. No one can run far enough, behave badly enough, or embrace ideas wild enough to become separated from God's love. Grace is without conditions. Where love and acceptance are accompanied by conditions, grace has not yet arrived. The gospel is about radical, disturbing, hilarious grace. To be with God is to be at home. To all who are away from home, word comes that the front door is always, always, open. The gospel really is good news.

The ministry of the gospel is more about laughing or crying while experiencing joy than about biting our lips while doing a duty. What could be more enjoyable than finding a woman who sees herself as unlovable and helping her to discover that she is loved with an incomprehensible love? How could time be better spent than sitting with a fellow who has become bitter about everything and introducing him to the God who can melt away bitterness and replace it with hope?

I had always thought of the obligation to share a Christian witness as an unwelcome demand to repeat a series of scripture passages in a certain sequence I could never remember and then to press a person to say, "I believe that." I have never liked to do that. I was not any good at it. How wrong! Witness is just that: talking about what is most important in life; saying to a person, "Let me tell you how I messed up, and God took the mess and did wonders with it. If you are ever in a mess, God can do the same for you."

Missions no longer means going somewhere I do not want to go and doing something I do not want to do or I cannot do. Being on mission means having a good time—the joy of seeing a person lost in life discover the way to live, the happiness of watching a person clad in rags put on a coat that stills the shivers and gives warmth, the festivity of helping an individual who thought life was over discover that it is just beginning. "Bear one another's burdens, and so fulfill the law of Christ." Yes.

Maybe the dimension of faith that changed and continues to change most dramatically for me was/is a recognition of the nature of the church. Be done with thoughts of buildings, programs, budgets, buses, and meetings. See people, all kinds of people.

More and more I think of the gathered church as a religious counterpart to that Canterbury pub described by Chaucer as a spot where pilgrims came and went to swap their stories of pilgrimage. Followers of Christ regularly get together to break bread, drink some wine, retell God's story, and talk to each other about their own successes and failures, hurts and joys, despair and hope—to cry together and laugh together, to celebrate and grieve, to unload burdens and to pick up burdens.

As church people, our identity is unmistakable. We do not need nametags. We are lovers who at times have been in love with things more than persons, with bondage more than freedom, with religion more than Christ. All of us desperately want to be loved. Some of us want to be more loving.

Worship, that primal activity of people of faith, the worship of God—the central activity of the church—is a celebration of love. By hymns and prayers, litanies and confessions, we try to speak of our love for God. By scripture readings, sermons, and communion, we learn of God's love for us. By intercessions and offerings, we express our love for others and resolve to channel the adrenalin of compassion stirred by divine worship into specific acts of service aimed at meeting human needs. Worship is a festival of love. The church is made up of lovers *and* strugglers. For few has faith come easily; for all the application of faith to live is fraught with difficulty. Our patron saint, if we are honest, is that nameless man in the gospels who said to Christ, "Lord, I believe, help my unbelief."

Remember Vincent van Gogh's question, "Does the road go up hill all the way?" The artist spoke our line. God's messenger responds succinctly, "Yes, to the very end." Like van Gogh, we also want to know, "And will the journey take all day long?" We are not surprised, however, when the messenger says, "From morning to night my friend."

Faithfulness replaces success as the goal of those who meet as church. No one claims to have arrived. Everybody just wants to be on the right road, knowing full well that the journey will involve struggling with tough decisions that have to be made and difficult actions that have to be taken as well as struggling with important questions that will never be answered.

We are lovers and strugglers. We are graceful people, individuals who have been touched by grace and cannot sit still until all people have been touched by grace. Our only hope for being church for others is grace. God knows we are not perfect. We are not patient. We do not come close to being divine. By God's grace, though, we have worth, meaning, joy, and promise. We are blessed, and we can bless.

We are heaven bent on building a community of grace. We are dead sure that if we ever want to be anything but a community of grace, we might as well cease to exist because we have already stopped being the church of Jesus Christ whom the author of the fourth Gospel referred to as "grace upon grace."

Most of us have been angry at the church at one time or another. Some of us have turned our backs on it. For others the verdict is not yet in. All of us have solid reasons for these reactions. Hear this, though—it is a word from God—we cannot give up on the church. If we do not like what it has been or what it is, fine. But we can't abandon Christ's vision or God's mission. With God's help, we simply have to do better, and we cannot do better without God's help.

From the small group retreats of the 1960s comes a story that serves me as a definition of mission. A leader handed a "Dixie" cup to the person seated at his side, explaining that the paper cup was a symbol of the church. "Do to it what you think needs to be done to the church, tell us why, and then pass it to the next person in the circle."

The first individual handled the cup carefully, then bent the lip of the cup at intervals indicating the church's need to be more flexible. Another person took a pencil and punched holes into the sides of the cup, speaking of his desire for the church to open up and better see the world around it. One man did not have to speak at all; his actions spoke for him. With obvious anger and resentment, he tore the cup into small pieces and defiantly hurled the pieces across the room. What the next person had planned to do and say, nobody ever knew. She got down on her hands and knees and crawled around the room meticulously picking up each piece of the torn-apart cup and lovingly trying to put it all back together.

A church has been handed to you. It belongs to God, of course, but Northminster is in your hands. With the gift, the blessing, comes responsibility, the challenge to bless. What will you do with it?

My South African friend had the appropriate benediction for that meeting years ago, for this sermon this morning, and for all efforts to sketch a guiding vision for the future of this congregation. Helped by the apostle Paul, he prayed that we would bear each other's burdens and thus fulfill the law of Christ—and he called it a privilege. Let it be, O God, let it be. Amen.

13.
Coming Home

Psalm 23
Luke 15:11-24

C. Welton Gaddy

(I delivered this sermon in the morning worship service of Northminster Church on 17 January 1993, prior to the installation of the church's first pastor that afternoon.)

Back in December, on my first Monday morning here in Monroe, I showed up at the church building before anyone else had arrived. No problem. On the night before, Cathe Nixon had instructed me on how to turn off the security system. Well, there was a problem. That little box of buttons by the front door did not look the same to me on Monday morning as it had on the previous evening. I punched in the numbers of the code and hit what I thought was the deactivating button, but the system did not shut down. Hurriedly, I did it all again, though, just in case I had misunderstood Cathe's instructions. This time I hit a different button to turn off the system.

As I was repeating this same sequence of actions for the fourth time, the alarm began to sound. Then came that booming pre-recorded voice that sounds like God but engenders hellish feelings. Not knowing what else to do, I returned to my car, sat down, and waited to see who would show up first.

Before too long I am sure, though I felt like it was on my first year's anniversary, a policeman arrived. I explained what had happened, assuring him that though this was my first morning here I knew both the code and password to the security system. After the two of us entered the building, I punched in the code again. This time it worked. The deafening siren fell silent.

The young police officer explained that he had to fill out a report on his visit, and this required me to answer some questions. After writing down my name, he asked for my address. I said, "I don't know it." He then asked for my phone number, and again I said, "I don't know it."

The fellow epitomized disbelief. Wanting to ask me something I did know, he inquired about the address and the phone number of the church. I told him I did not know the address, but I was sure the phone number was on my telephone, but it was not. Looking me straight in the eye, the policeman said, "Do you reckon you know the date of your birth?" I said, "I think I do, but I'm not sure."

Then came the cavalry. Actually, Don walked in. What a relief! But it was shortlived. My pastoral colleague looked at me studiously and then with feigned outrage said to the policeman, "Who is this man? What is he doing here?"

Finally, the ordeal was over. We all laughed, at least I think I did. Don and I sat down and talked about where I live, my address, my phone number, and a lot of other topics as well.

It is terrible not to have a home or to feel like you do not have a home. It is wonderful to have a home and to feel good about being there.

The sermon for this morning is about being at home. As I offer it to God and to you, I want to express thanks to the psalmist of the Old Testament, appreciation to the author of the fourth Gospel in the New Testament, and apologies to Thomas Wolfe.

Many years ago, I was so struck by the title of Wolfe's classic work, *You Can't Go Home Again*, that I believed it without question. I made a mistake in judgment—so did Wolfe, in my opinion. The holy scriptures have helped me to better understand the truth about home.

Oh, to be sure, the title of Wolfe's book signals a measure of truth. If going home again means returning to a specific geographical locale and finding all the people and places just as you left them, you cannot go home again—not even after a one day stay away from home.

When I go back to the town of my childhood and youth, I never cease to be amazed that the streets I remembered as long and wide are in reality narrow and short. A vacant lot that once seemed like a duplicate of Yankee Stadium was no more than a tiny square of dust. The forest in which I roamed as Tarzan consisted of only three or four trees. The arena in which year after year I successfully competed in the Final Four was a worn-out patch of grass under an apple tree that overhung a basketball goal as crooked as it was rusty. Often I have been tempted to parrot Thomas Wolfe and sigh nostalgically, "You can't go home again." But, you *can* go home again. Home is not about plots of earth, dusty or paved. Home is not about streets and buildings. Home is about relationships.

In Jesus' parable of the prodigal son, the wayward boy arrived home the moment he walked into the open arms of his waiting father, not when he finally entered his father's house. If no one but the elder brother had been around when the younger son showed up, the penitent pilgrim would not even have been home once he arrived at his destination.

Home is about unique relationships with special people. It really is a matter of the heart. Being at home means interacting with individuals who accept you for who you are, love you as you are, forgive you when you do wrong, fail to count the number of times they allow you to try again, and shower you with mercy. To experience home is to be welcomed even when you are not vey nice to be around and to be cared for even though you have been uncaring. Sure, at home people challenge your misbehavior, seek to help you correct mistakes, and urge you to be all you can be—but all of that is done with sensitive love.

Biblical writers associated home with the most important relationship in life. Being at home meant being with God. Psalm 90 begins, "O Lord, you have always been our home." In the Today's English Version of Psalm 23, the poem directed to God concludes, "Surely goodness and love will be with me all my life; and your house will be my home as long as I live." According to John's gospel, Jesus prepared a way for all people to be present with God, to be at home.

No doubt you are aware of this truth about home experientially, if not theologically. Like me, you have been in familiar places surrounded by people you have known for years and felt like a stranger. Conversely, at times you have found yourself relating to persons with such intimacy that you knew you were at home, regardless of how long you had been there. Place was inconsequential. All that mattered were the sound of the voices you could hear, the look in the eyes of those speaking, and the spirit that swept over you.

During the past several weeks, many of you have spoken to me about your involvement in Northminster Church. Time and time again you have used family terminology. Before I returned to Monroe after accepting your invitation to serve as your pastor, Derward Culp called me and talked of his discovery of family here. On my first Sunday morning as your pastor, Patti Bateman greeted me with a kiss on the cheek and the words, "Welcome to the family." Around a dinner table one evening,

Carol Ann Tubbs spoke of coming to Northminster as coming home. At the church business meeting last Sunday evening, Priscilla Asbury talked about Northminster being a family and functioning as a family. Such comments have continued repeatedly.

I need to let you know how it is for me. Years have passed, over a decade at least, since Judy and I have felt at home spiritually speaking. Across these years I have returned to places of spiritual significance in my past only to sense the devastation of those first century Jews rummaging around the ravages of the Holy City after it was sacked by the Romans. Like those spiritual kinfolks, I mourned. I have attended denominational meetings only to sit down amid people whose names I knew well but whose mindsets made me feel like a complete stranger. I have worshiped and preached in beautiful buildings located behind impressive signage that identified them as the meeting places of churches only to depart with no desire ever to return to them again. I have listened to people pontificate about doctrinal dogma and felt my spirit scratched by the nagging hunch that if those people are right, I am wrong; if they are "in," I am "out."

Frankly, people whom I most trust have told me that my view of the Church has always been idealistic and unrealistic. I have to admit that I have believed the Church to be better than I have experienced it being. For a long time that belief did not waver. When it did, though, the shaking was profound. Insincerity, rejection, and just plain meanness among people who claimed to congregate in Christ's name prompted disappointment, hurt, anger, and resentment within me. As a child of the Church, I felt I had lost my spiritual home.

Thankfully, during this period of time as never before in my life, I became aware of the nature of God and the truth of the gospel. My beliefs did not take shape around instructions from family members or lectures from respected teachers. My convictions clustered around the God and the gospel I met in the Bible and saw in Jesus. My personal faith was fine most of the time, but I missed a family of faith desperately. I prepared myself to be a spiritual nomad, a perpetual itinerant in search of a community of faith that I presumed to be an impossibility.

In recent days, through the actions of your pastor search committee and several of my long-time friends and by the grace of God, we—you and I—have been brought together. Almost from the start, I sensed something different about this community of faith. As my dialogue with members of the search committee stretched across the weeks and delved deeper into various subjects, I found myself wanting to trust again, to believe again that church is possible. As usual, Judy was ahead of me. She seems to know good instinctively. I have to analyze it before I can feel it.

In one of our meetings, I asked the pastor search committee for an agreement aimed at making our conversations beneficial regardless of their outcome. If they decided upon someone other than me to recommend for this pastorate, they would tell me why in detail. Similarly, if I terminated our discussions, I would do so by sharing specific reasons for my decision. On the other hand, if we moved forward, we would share with each other the reasons for our coming together. We agreed.

The committee kept its part of that deal via a letter from Craig Henry that I have in my files. This morning I want to keep my part of that agreement by sharing with you the specifics of your corporate life that attracted Judy and me here and served as media for God's call to us to come here.

One caveat is necessary. After acquaintances and friends have said to me in disbelief, "You are going to return to a pastorate!" two questions have dominated their interests in this church. "Where is it?" came first. By far the most frequently asked question, though, was "What size is it?" To talk honestly about my understanding of why we are together, I have to leave both of those inquiries unaddressed. In a search for a real church, size and place are virtually irrelevant.

Your pastor search committee represented the Northminster congregation with excellence. Early on I liked them—every one of them—and felt spiritual kinship with them. I knew if the rest of you were anything at all like these people, Judy and I would be at home here. As I began to meet you individually, I liked you—all of you. So did Judy. I know there must be some members of this church who are pains in the neck and anatomical points south, but right now they are without names. Then, too, I like and appreciate the ministers you had already invited to serve here. Don and Cathe are special people—a little crazy, but special—with whom I look forward to working.

Here are some of the other traits of Northminster that make me feel at home:

•your courage to act on basic convictions

•your willingness to work physically as well as to give financially to translate dreams into realities and faith into action

•your commitment to the priority of the meaningful worship of God

•your interest in the civic and social community

•your appreciation for diversity

•your realization that being Baptist is more basic than affiliating with one particular group or convention

•your disinterest in narrow sectarianism and your devotion to honest ecumenism

•your enthusiasm

•your sense of humor and love of laughter

•your intention to be led even when that is uncomfortable and to be leaders even when that is controversial

•your insistence on biblical preaching from a free pulpit

•your inclusiveness

•your ability to take the gospel seriously without becoming somber people

•your free thinking

•your desire to disagree with each other vigorously without violating your respect and love for each other minimally

•your passion for excellence

•your recognition of the human condition that has had only one exception—thus your willingness to extend grace to all who make mistakes, err, mess up, fail, miss the mark, sin

•your belief that the gospel is good news for everybody—no exceptions

•your delight in breaking the bread and sharing the cup of communion.

I do not want to be unrealistic about who you are and what we can do and become together. At the same time, I do not want to give up the possibility of us inching ever nearer to the New Testament vision of church. When we fail at being church for others or mess up in acting as priests to each other, as we will, I want us to renew our efforts to do better. The inevitability of shortcomings of the spirit must not be used as a rationale by which we can be comfortable settling for less than with God's help is possible.

As your pastor, I want to challenge you, offer biblical counsel, lead you, and love you through failures and accomplishments as you make some basic decisions such as

•how to move from the vision of beginning a new congregation to a vision of how best to serve as a congregation while maintaining in service the same intensity of passion that you brought to the inception of your corporate life

•how to retain a focus on the good news of the gospel of love and peace in the face of mounting problems that could become major distractions

•how to preserve the sense of family without yielding to the lure of exclusiveness

•how to handle constructive criticism from those who love you and want to see you succeed as well as from those who condemn you and want to see you fail

•how to proceed in nurturing an institution that allows you to carry out your mission without falling into the trap of preserving the institution at the expense of losing sight of the mission

•how to avoid protecting the nature of this church without developing prejudices toward others who are different

•how to continue to implement the concept of every member of the church functioning as a minister amid the inevitable tendency to assign ministry to only certain persons

•how to maintain an allegiance to and contacts with the larger religious community when pressing concerns here at home threaten to consume our time and energies

•how to preserve a particular style of worship and ministry without being more devoted to the style than to the God for whom the style is to bring honor and glory

•how to stay on course during periods when duty seems more prominent than joy, when the journey must be continued without enthusiasm

•how to follow as well as how to lead.

Well, that is it: a sermon with somewhere around thirty points, but a message pulsating with the specifics of a fellowship that feels like home.

The story is told of how the noted Dutch theologian Henri Nouwen has lived with the fantasy that every time he lands at an airport he will be met by someone he knows crying, "Hey, Henri." Predictably, Nouwen has known a lot of disappointments. Each time that he deplanes and no familiar figure meets him, though, Nouwen tells himself, "It's alright. When I get home my friends will be there." Out of that thought of consolation, Nouwen came to a wonderful conclusion about the nature of heaven. He said, "Heaven is going to be like that. God will be there and will say, 'Hey, Henri, how was it? Let's see your slides.' "

Not only is Nouwen's vision an apt way to understand heaven; it also provides insight into the nature of the church. Church—any church, Northminster Church—is to be a fellowship of God's people to which anyone can come at any time and hear the greeting, "Hey, come on in. Welcome home. Tell us about your journey."

My hunch is that before Judy and I got here, some of you wondered aloud to each other, "Do you suppose we could forego asking to see their slides." I understand. However you answered that question, though, you were ready with other words.

Joining you on our pilgrimage as Northminster Church has been like walking into a gathering of people who immediately seem like family and hearing the greeting, "Hey, Welton and Judy. Come on in. Welcome home." God knows, and I want you to know, it is good to be home!

14.
Shepherd and Sheep

John 21:15-22

Frank Stagg

(On Sunday afternoon, 17 January 1993, Frank Stagg preached the installation sermon for the first pastor of Northminster Church.)

Carlyle Marney (whom I first knew when we were seminary students in Louisville, Kentucky) many years ago, in what I take to be one of his finest books, *Structures of Prejudice,* chose to close it with these lines: "Our hope requires the recovery of the personal in relation. Nothing else matters—much."[1]

The great Jewish philosopher-theologian Martin Buber taught us that the truly personal is possible only in relation with other persons, and that the language of true personhood is not I-it (subject speaking to object) but I-thou (subject meeting subject).

I believe that John 21 puts into focus many of the things that belong to this perspective and what I take to be basically what Church is all about, the personal in relation: in relation to God, not as an "it," but in personal terms; in relationship with ourselves, for that is a basic relationship; and in relationship with other persons, never forgetting that they are, indeed, persons and not things.

The Gospel of John seems to come to its intended conclusion at the end of Chapter 20. There is explicit the goal toward which it was moving, the confession of Jesus as "Lord and God" (v. 28). Then comes the "sign off" of the author as he summed up what had been his method and goal (vv. 30-31). The Gospel does not end there, however. Had this Gospel come to us ending with Chapter 20, we would not have had any sense of its incompletion. If Chapter 21 had not been there, even as an addendum, we would have missed a lot!

John 21 is usually called an appendix to the Gospel. Had the author been some covert Louisiana Cajun, he may have written this off as "Lagniappe." But, however defined, much in Chapter 21 should speak to us on an occasion like this.

There are two basic commands in the passage, each in variation. One command says in effect: "If you love me, then express it in terms of my people. Feed my lambs. Shepherd my sheep. Feed my sheep" (vv. 15-17). Then the other command, also in variation, first says simply: "Follow me" (v. 19). Then, in view of the differing circumstances under which we individually fulfill our calling, he said in effect: "How others may fair is not your affair. *You* follow me whatever the cost."

Well, to follow another person, we have to know something about that person and where that one is going. We hear the song, "I Have Decided to Follow Jesus," and many people think they have followed him just by singing it. No! Many do not even bother to see which way Jesus went! This passage does instruct us about Jesus and which way he was going.

Seven of the disciples, with apparent resignation so far as was the dream they had pursued for a few short years, turned back to their older vocation. They got into their boat and went fishing in Lake Galilee. They fished all night and caught nothing; then Jesus appeared on the shore at daybreak. He called out to them, fed them, probed them, and then commissioned them.

From one perspective, we may say, "Well, there's no surprise that Jesus went to the trouble of going out there to the lake and finding the seven. These were prize disciples! You know he could not afford to lose them: Saint Peter, Saint John, Saint Thomas, Saint James." Well, they were not saints then. They were not blue ribbon or blue chip people then.

They had a worth, but not an achieved worth. It is the worth that belongs to humanity by virtue of the fact that we simply have been brought into this world. We should see these men not as blue ribbon, not as a blue chip group, but just fallible followers of Jesus in the making.

There was Thomas, the doubter. He defined the terms on which his faith could be commanded. He demanded tangible proof of Jesus' resurrection.

There was Nathaniel, known as a man without guile, but he was also a man not without his provincialism. On one occasion he said, "What good or can anything good come out of Nazareth?" (John 1:46).

There were the brothers James and John. On one occasion (Luke 9:49-50), John reported to Jesus, very proudly awaiting praise, "We saw some casting out demons in your name, and we told them to stop." Jesus said, "You stop telling them to stop." Exclusion was to be replaced by inclusion. On another occasion when they were going through Samaria, one of the villages did not put out the red carpet for them. John, known later as the beloved, said to Jesus, "Shall we call down fire from heaven and burn them up?"

One time (Mark 10:35-38) James and John came to Jesus saying, "We have something to ask of you." "What is it?" Jesus responded. "When you come into your kingdom, grant that we may have the top spots in your cabinet—one at your left and one at your right." Jesus said, "You don't know what you are asking for. You don't have a smattering of an idea what it is to be at my left and my right."

There was Peter, esteemed when the four Gospels were written. The Gospels told it like it really was. One time after Jesus spoke of his own identity and vocation, Peter undertook to correct him on these basic things. In effect, Jesus said, "Just get out of my way." There was that final scene before Jesus' death when three times they asked Peter about Jesus and he said, "I don't know him; I don't know the man." Finally, reverting to his fisherman language, Peter swore and said, "I don't know the man" (Matt 26:72-74).

The disciples were not a blue ribbon group, but they were people. They were persons, at best diamonds in the rough. Jesus went out there and met them at daybreak to include them, not to exclude them.

Inclusion was the pattern with Jesus. He got into trouble by including the rejects of culture and piety: the Samaritan, the gentile, the leper, the lame, the blind, the deaf, and women. In defense of his including many persons who were supposed to be excluded by the standards of the time, Jesus said, "The physician goes to the sick." Jesus came to seek and to save sinners. Jesus included individuals not on the basis of achieved merits, but on the basis of intrinsic worth—the worth that belongs to every human being regardless of the extent to which that human being may have wasted that treasure or it had been wasted or destroyed by others. That was his pattern.

It is unfortunate, a grief, indeed a disgrace, that much of the life of the Church has not been in following Jesus in the pattern of inclusion but rather exclusion. This practice started in the very earliest days. One of the biggest controversies calling for a church council, as recorded in Acts 15, was an argument about circumcision, whether or not people could be included if they had not met certain cultic rights—an all-important issue for those who preferred exclusion over inclusion. Then the Church, after being on the defensive for a time, finally, especially in the fourth century under Constantine, became power people with the power of the empire behind them.

Here is another story. The first ecumenical conference in Nicea in 325 C.E. was called and presided over by a man who was said to have converted to Christianity. In all likelihood, however, Christianity was converted to Constantine. Constantine changed the Cross from the sign under which one may give life to the sign under which one may take life. Under this perversion, the Church turned to excluding its own members, even killing some of them.

There were Athanasius of Alexandria and Arius, with their theological differences. The powers, religious and political, were behind Athanasius; so Arius was excluded and anathematized.

In the same century, Augustine had the power with him—not necessarily right or truth, but power. Pelagius went to Rome and was shocked by the immorality he saw among the clergy as well as the laity. When he insisted upon reform, they opposed him on the grounds that he taught human perfectibility (the Sermon on the Mount could be so understood!). They finally excluded him in favor of the theological baggage that we have inherited from Augustine, with its preoccupation with Adam, even though there is no trace that any prophet or Jesus ever referred to Adam. Seemingly we do not know that we are not called to be bellhops; we could put down such luggage if we chose to. Worst of all, exclusion became the pattern following Constantine.

William Tyndale, a brilliant scholar, was the first person to translate a Greek testament into English. His work did not please the power in England where church and state were one and the same, just two sides of the same coin. Tyndale was caught and burned at the stake by the Church.

The Reformation was largely the rearranging of prejudices, where Protestants excluded or even killed one another. John Calvin gained power in Geneva when he sanctioned the burning of Servetus. Not one person in a million knows the alleged heresy of Servetus. Zwingli and the city council had the Anabaptist Felix Manz drowned in the Limmat River in Zurich.

On and on it goes. In our time, as Southern Baptists, there was C. H. Toy. Because he had an education and a probing mind, ahead of his day, he was exiled from us and had to finish his days at Harvard. There was

Whitsitt who wrote an encyclopedia article on Baptists that no scholar to-day challenges, but it did not please the powers. He was forced to resign the presidency of our first Southern Baptist seminary. All the way down to people like Paul Simmons, the record is one of excluding.

What about today? In the sixty years and more that I have been called a minister, there have been so many exclusions. There was the racial issue, where the color of one's skin was used as justification for excluding. Gender is still a basic criterion by which some exclude others, either totally or from the highest exercise of their gifts.

There is another issue upon us now that we are not comfortable even mentioning. We will not settle it here, but neither will it go away—the gay community. Sixty years ago I knew the word "homosexual," and that was all I knew about it. When evidence came about homosexuality, we thought there were just a few gays in the whole world, and they were way out yonder. Of course, we knew about Plato and Julius Ceasar, but that was another age. Now, that is not so. We know that homosexuals are not just far away; they are near. They are not just strangers; they are our kin and friends or the kin and friends of our kin and friends. We have to cope with this. Anyone who has the wisdom, grace, and courage to lead us through this issue will do us service. But it is not enough simply to be pejorative and say, "Get away."

We still have the divisive issue of religious rites. One of the strangest situations I have ever heard of arose a few years ago in a neighboring state. Alien immersion was the litmus test—how you stood on that issue determined whether you were acceptable or not. The local association was in its annual meeting, hosted by the First Baptist Church in a county seat town. In the first session of this meeting, the credentials committee made a recommendation that the association adopted—resolving not to seat messengers from the host church, in effect, to exclude the host church from the association. The association was "gracious" enough to extend an invitation to those unseated messengers to remain in their own house as guests of the association, however.

If we want to follow Jesus, we had better ask: "Who was He? What were his values? What were his principles? Which way was he going? Was his basic disposition to find some excuse to exclude, or was it to find commonality—at least love by which we can include one another?"

It is interesting—the order in which Jesus approached those seven disciples that early morning at the seashore, "Lads, have you caught anything?" After following his lead and catching a whole host of fish, the disciples got to shore and found a fire and breakfast waiting for them. Jesus fed them before he preached to them, before he probed them. That was his order.

You do not say, "Listen to the sermon, and then we'll feed you." Jesus first fed them. There is something more to it than that. He not only began with their hunger and then went on to more important things. Jesus followed the principle that you do not have to await agreement before eating together. One pattern is that only when we find ourselves in agreement can we can take communion together. Jesus' pattern was "Let's sit down and eat, and we'll talk about it."

Then there is the test Jesus gave. The disciples would fail him in many ways. Their record could hardly have been poorer. When Jesus put them to test, though, he did not give them an examination in systematic theology or biblical theology. He did not ask for their credentials in terms of religious rites. Jesus said, "Do you love me?" (John 21).

Peter knew he had no record to stand on. But he said, "You know, Lord, in spite of everything, you know I do." Jesus followed again and again, "Do you love me? Do you love me? Do you love me?" There is no doubt that Jesus loved these men, or he would not have been there. The question is, did they love Jesus? If they did, they had enough as basis for persons in relation.

You can take it from there and meet any question, any issue that is proper to persons in relation. "Do you love me?" Then Jesus moved on to the expression of it.

"If you love me, then feed my lambs. If you love me, shepherd my sheep. If you love me, feed my sheep. If you love me, do something for my people, those dear to me." According to Matthew 25, Jesus had taught that "In that you did it to those in need, you did it to me; and in what you failed to do to them, you failed to do to me." That is his test.

Then, Jesus said to Peter, "Follow me." He warned him that to do so meant that down the road rejection and martyrdom awaited him. Peter turned to one called the beloved and asked, "What about him, what about this one?" Jesus said, "What if he would not only escape martyrdom but even escape death and live until I come; what is that to you? Your calling is yours, and you are to fulfill it. Whether or not you observe it is not to be determined by how others fare. That's not your affair. You follow me; shepherd my sheep."

It is a joy to me that we have Northminster Church that we esteem and for which we have such affection, a church with so many gifts, dedicated gifts. It is a joy to me that we have Judy and Welton Gaddy with their many gifts and dedication. It is such a happy union when these are brought together as here in this relationship of persons, as shepherds and sheep. Let us commit ourselves to the Chief Shepherd and to one another as persons in relationship. Little else matters.

Endnote

[1]Carlyle Marney, *Structures of Prejudice: An Approach to Understanding and Dealing with Prejudice in Culture* (New York: Abingdon Press, 1961) 245.

Epilogue
Living at Home

Eventually a moment arrives when people who have come home face the challenge of settling in and living at home. A different set of emotions surfaces at this point. The original determination to get home that sustained the long journey to the eagerly-sought destination and the initial rush of excitement that accompanied an arrival at home recede. Anxiety and resolution develop in reaction to questions about how to live at home: Will this work? Will I grow weary of being at home or become disillusioned about the joy of home? Can all of us who are here get along together? How will we make decisions? Should we protect this fellowship at all costs, or must we risk vulnerability for the sake of ministry? What should we do about relating to an extended family? How can we continue to kindle the warmth of our enthusiasm and sustain the strength of our commitment to inclusiveness? Can we maintain our home without becoming so preoccupied with preserving the institution that we cease acting with compassion in relation to every individual person?

Ernest Campbell once talked about the prodigal son in Jesus' parable who returned home after a long, tough time away. Exultant rejoicing properly ruled the day when the fellow got back to his family. What a wonderful sound to the elderly father's ears when, in an exclamation of relief and a burst of jubilation, his youngest son shouted, "I'm home!" Most everyone understands that sensation. As Ernie reflected on the situation, though, he raised an interesting question related to the son's life at home. How would the father have felt if a year or two later his youngest son was still bolting around the house shouting, "I'm home!"? Undoubtedly the unparalleled joy he experienced upon his son's arrival would give way to grievous disappointment. Ernie made the important point that a time comes when the celebration appropriate to arriving at home must give way to taking care of the business involved in living at home.

Our family of faith continues to laugh and talk about our journey home. We give thanks regularly for our life together. That does not mean, though, that every moment we share is filled with sweetness and light. Occasionally we feel the chill of the darkness from which we came. From time to time, bitterness and cynicism bred by old betrayals and disappointments push their way into our corporate consciousness. Periodically we even needle each other as a result of a distrust we learned in the past. Now and then we have to resist vigorously a temptation to practice the kind of exclusiveness in our fellowship and narrowness in our vision that we have disliked in other structures. At times, we fail. Letting go of previous hurts can be surprisingly difficult.

We like who we are and enjoy what we are doing. So, we wrestle with the problem of unhealthy pride. It is like walking a tight rope. We have good reasons to be proud of our fellowship, but we have to remember that God brought us into being, that we are not the only people with whom God is pleased, and that God has more for us to do than we have yet done.

Challenges loom large on the horizon toward which we are moving. What will we do about additional buildings? How much of our family's finances should we give to missions projects outside of our fellowship, and how much should we devote to our own church's involvements when our church itself is a mission? What kind of alliances do we want to form in order to increase the breadth of our relationships and the outreach of our ministry? As Baptists, how can we distinguish ourselves from others who claim the same name but reject historic Baptist principles and behave as another kind of people? How can we preserve the distinct identity of our home while welcoming a wide variety of new family members into it?

Our community of faith finds the corporate worship of God to be the strongest foundation upon which to build a response to these challenges and the best context in which to do that work. As we meet to worship God, we discover how to balance a healthy pride with a pride in need of challenge, thanksgiving for our past with openness to the future, and celebrations of successes with reasons for repentance. So, conscientiously and congregationally, we prepare for each weekly experience of corporate worship as if it were the first time we have been together and participate in that service as if it were the last time we would be together.

Northminster Church considers the worship of God to be its most important work—praising God and catching a glimpse of how to serve God in the world. In our worship of God, we remember who we are and why we are.

On several occasions, different individuals have engaged me in virtually the same conversation. While discussing decisions to be made, people to be embraced, and ministries to be initiated by our fellowship, attention turns to the troublesome difficulties of functioning as a New Testament church in general and specifically to the potential problems involved in our congregation acting redemptively. Invariably someone says, "I know we are going to face hardships, but we have no choice. We must act." When I press the conversationalist in search of more understanding about the urgency and adamancy of this response, she says, "Look, for many of us, this is our last hope related to the church. If we can't be church here, a lot of us will just completely give up on the whole idea of church."

The intensity involved in such conversations reflects the intentional nature of the Northminster congregation. Some folks refer to our fellowship as "the church of the strong will." Personally, however, I think a more accurate title is "providence church." At every major juncture in the fellowship's life, the will and provisions of God have run ahead of the vision and readiness of the people involved. Once the church has seen God's will, though, the exercise of a strong will and determined actions within the congregation is without question.

No person in the Northminster family of faith holds any illusions about institutional perfection. God knows (and we know all too well) our weaknesses, but we are serious about trying to be God's people.

During the installation service for the new pastor, Don Nixon spoke words that exquisitely capture Northminster's concept of self-identity as well as its commitment to ministry:

> Welton, before you become part of this colorful collection, there are some things you need to know. None of us here are real pretty sights . . . not as clean as we need or know to be. . . . We have smudges and blemishes that religious people would run from . . . but we recognize those inadequacies and are daily striving to be different. . . . So . . . don't come along if you are expecting a pageant of total beauty.

> None of us are totally grown . . . but we are moving through that process and are open to all stages that must occur for that goal of fulfillment to be obtained. So don't come along if you are looking only for a band of mature adult merrymakers.

> We don't have a lot to offer in the way of possessions, religious acceptance, vast numbers of people, prestige, or financial comfort. . . . What

is here has come from a blending of the talents, the commitment to the
search for truth, and the willingness to offer lives to God no matter
what the cost. . . .

And if, deep within your soul, you have a longing for a small group of
dirty struggling spirits to walk beside you, to share the load you must
carry, to lovingly divide with you their very rations and gains and allow
you the freedom of beginning on a new journey . . . then, welcome
home my brother. . . . We've been looking for you.

Northminster Church is committed to living out a mission by which God
makes of us a mission: to relate redemptively to all people, live as a family, and welcome into our community of faith every person in need of a
spiritual home.

Many years ago, in one of my favorite books of all time, Howard
Thurman wrote words about a church that made my heart beat faster and
caused my hopes to soar. I desperately wanted to experience what Thurman had experienced in a church where he once was the pastor so that
I could claim his words as my own. Somewhere, sometime, I had given
up on that possibility. Then, the God of surprises surprised me.

As I write the concluding words of this volume, I have no idea what
the future will hold, but, I do know the present. Right now, mine is the
joy of using Howard Thurman's autobiographical confessions autobio-
graphically.

There has not been a single day since the beginning of the church that
I have not been moved by its spirit. . . . For a breathless moment in
time, a little group of diverse peoples was caught up in a dream as old
as life and as new as a hope that just emerges on the horizon of becoming (a person).[1]

Living at home is as joyful an experience as coming home. Thanks
be to God!

Endnote

[1]Howard Thurman, *With Head and Heart: The Autobiography of Howard
Thurman* (New York: Harcourt, Brace, Jovanovich, 1979) 162.